The
CAPRICORN
Path

YOUR DAILY 2026 HOROSCOPE GUIDE

AMANDA M CLARKE

Copyright © Amanda M Clarke 2026
KORU Publishing

All rights reserved. All content, materials, and intellectual property in this book or any other platform owned by Koru Publishing are protected by copyright laws. This includes text, images, graphics, videos, audio, software, and any other form of content that may be produced by Koru Publishing.

No part of this content may be reproduced, distributed, or transmitted in any form or by any means without the prior written permission of Koru Publishing. This means that you cannot copy, reproduce, or use any of the content in this book for commercial or personal purposes without the express written consent of Koru Publishing.

Unauthorized use of any copyrighted material owned by Koru Publishing may result in legal action being taken against you. Koru Publishing reserves the right to pursue all available legal remedies against any individual or entity found to be infringing on its copyright.

In summary, Koru Publishing © 2024 holds exclusive rights to all the content produced by it, and any unauthorized use of such content will result in legal action.

KORU Publishing

KORU (Maori,NZ)
A symbol of spiritual growth and spiritual connection.

Rocky Point Townhouse, CHRISTMAS ISLAND, Western Australia 6798

More on the Bookshelves at
www.theliteraryoracle.com

Disclaimer: The Capricorn Path: Your daily 2026 horoscope guide book provides information on astrological readings and intuative interpretations, it is not intended as a substitute for professional advice, diagnosis, or treatment. The information contained in this book is provided for educational and entertainment purposes only and is not meant to be taken as specific advice for individual circumstances. The author and publisher make no representations or warranties with respect to the accuracy or completeness of the contents of this book and specifically disclaim any implied warranties of merchantability or fitness for a particular purpose. The reader should always consult with a licensed professional for any specific concerns or questions. The author and publisher shall not be liable for any loss or damage caused or alleged to have been caused, directly or indirectly, by the information contained in this book. The use of this book is

More from Amanda Clarke
The Literary Oracle
www.theliteracyoracle.com

The "Daily Guidance" series offers an innovative approach to finding spiritual wisdom and practical advice. Each book in the series is a unique tool designed for daily introspection and decision-making. Readers are invited to meditate on a question or seek general guidance for the day, then flip to a random page in the book. The page they land on provides a personalized message from various spiritual sources, such as angels, tarot, or spirit animals. With each turn of the page, these books deliver insightful, positive messages and mantras to inspire personal growth and provide clarity on life's daily challenges and decisions.

Other books in this series:-
The Angelic Oracles
Daily Angel Tarot Reading
Mystic Tarot Cat
Oracle of the Tarot Cat
Vibes Unveiled
Spirit Animal Oracle
Answers from the Oracles
Messages from the Angels

Supporting Indie Authors

Love your daily guidance? You can grab more of my books direct from The Literary Oracle:
www.theliteraryoracle.com

Buying direct means:
- Much better prices for you + free shipping.
- More support for me as an indie author
- More magical books in your hands

My books are also available worldwide through online bookstores, but direct purchases help keep the magic flowing.

Thank you for supporting indie creativity!

Welcome to The Capricorn Path: Your Daily 2026 Horoscope Guide — your steadfast, grounding companion for the year ahead. Crafted for the determined, disciplined, and quietly powerful Capricorn, this guide honours the way you move through life — with ambition, resilience, and a deep commitment to building something lasting.

Inside, you'll find daily horoscopes paired with affirmations designed to strengthen your natural gifts. Each reading is here to support you as you navigate 2026 with purpose — whether you're striving toward career goals, nurturing relationships, prioritising well-being, or laying foundations for long-term success.

This isn't about quick wins — it's about steady progress. As you turn each page, you'll gather clarity, encouragement, and grounded wisdom from the cosmos, guiding you to trust both your instincts and the path beneath your feet. Let this be the year you embrace patience, resilience, and the quiet magic of living in harmony with your true nature and the stars above.

The Answers You Seek

Are Within

January 2026

Capricorn
01 January 2026

Capricorn, the new year begins with the Moon highlighting your ambitions and personal goals. You're stepping into this year with determination, though a quiet part of you wonders if you've truly set the right intentions. Trust yourself—you've built resilience over the years. Today is not about rushing but about clarity. Take time to map out what you really want, even if it feels overwhelming. One focused step today can ripple into lasting change.

Affirmation & Gratitude

I am grateful for new beginnings, trusting the wisdom of my past to guide every step I take forward.

Capricorn
02 January 2026

You may feel a tension between responsibilities and your desire for freedom. It's okay to crave both stability and adventure. The stars show a nudge toward balancing duty with spontaneity—honoring obligations without losing sight of joy. A small act of self-care or play will ground you, preventing burnout. Remember, your worth isn't tied only to productivity. Notice what makes you smile today, even in the middle of serious work. That lightness will fuel your long-term vision.

Affirmation & Gratitude

I allow myself to enjoy the present moment, knowing balance makes me stronger and more effective in my path.

Capricorn
03 January 2026

Today emphasizes relationships, Capricorn. You may be asked to compromise or meet someone halfway. It's tempting to hold firm, but listening without judgment will open doors. The cosmos shows that partnerships—romantic, work, or family—will mirror back your own strengths and insecurities. This is a chance to practice patience and acceptance, especially if emotions run high. A meaningful connection today could teach you more about yourself than any solitary reflection. Speak honestly, but also listen deeply.

Affirmation & Gratitude

I am grateful for the lessons others bring into my life, teaching me patience, compassion, and deeper understanding.

Capricorn
04 January 2026

Your energy surges today as Mars fuels your drive. You might feel unstoppable, ready to conquer tasks or initiate new projects. But remember: pacing yourself is wise. The temptation to push past your limits could lead to unnecessary strain. Focus on strategy, not speed. Ask yourself what deserves your full energy versus what can wait. By channelling effort carefully, you'll build stronger results. Confidence grows when discipline meets ambition—a true Capricorn hallmark.

Affirmation & Gratitude

I honor my strength by pacing myself, knowing consistent effort leads to lasting success and fulfillment.

Capricorn
05 January 2026

The cosmos highlights your finances and resources today. You may feel the urge to make bold moves, like investing or reshaping budgets. Take a moment to review details before acting impulsively. Practicality is your natural strength—use it to ground any big financial ideas. Security matters, but so does knowing your money supports the life you want. Balance careful planning with trust in your instincts. Opportunities come to those who prepare.

Affirmation & Gratitude

I am grateful for abundance flowing into my life, and I use my resources wisely to support my true dreams.

Capricorn
06 January 2026

Rest becomes essential today, Capricorn. The stars suggest your mind may be racing with responsibilities, but your body is asking for stillness. Don't mistake slowing down as weakness—it's an act of strength. Recharge through reflection, journaling, or time in nature. Inspiration will come when you allow silence to speak. Your dreams or intuition may reveal clues about your next step, so stay open to subtle messages.

Affirmation & Gratitude

I honor my need for rest, knowing stillness restores my spirit and prepares me for the challenges ahead.

Capricorn
07 January 2026

The week closes with a burst of social energy. Friends or colleagues may seek your guidance, and you'll shine naturally as a leader. But remember, you don't need all the answers. Sometimes presence and encouragement are enough. Networking or connecting today could spark opportunities you didn't expect—stay open to casual conversations that may turn into golden doors. Your influence is growing, Capricorn. Step forward with both confidence and humility.

Affirmation & Gratitude

I am grateful for connections that inspire and uplift me, knowing shared energy creates growth and opportunity for all.

Capricorn
08 January 2026

Capricorn, today shines a light on your career and public image. You may find yourself recognized for past efforts, even if subtly. Someone notices your reliability and steady hand, and this can open a door you've been waiting for. Yet, don't let external validation distract from your inner compass. Ask yourself whether the opportunities ahead align with your long-term goals, not just your reputation. Integrity matters more than applause. Keep reminding yourself that success built on authenticity endures far longer than fleeting recognition.

Affirmation & Gratitude

I honor my achievements with humility, grateful that my work and integrity pave the way for future success.

Capricorn
09 January 2026

A wave of introspection stirs today. Old memories or unfinished business may resurface, urging you to address what's been tucked away. Avoid brushing aside uncomfortable emotions—there's healing waiting in acknowledgment. The stars reveal that by facing the past, you strengthen your resilience for the future. Closure doesn't always come from others; sometimes it comes from within. Journaling, meditation, or quiet reflection will help you untangle knots that still tug at your spirit. Trust this process—it's a gift of release.

Affirmation & Gratitude

I am grateful for my inner strength, and I release what no longer serves me to create space for peace.

Capricorn
10 January 2026

Relationships may feel intense today, with the Moon drawing focus to your emotional bonds. You might crave reassurance, but resist the urge to test those you love. Instead, lean into honest communication and vulnerability. Sharing your feelings won't make you weak—it deepens trust. The stars suggest a heartfelt conversation could unlock greater intimacy and understanding. Remember, Capricorn, your steadiness is a gift, but allowing others to see your softer side makes the bond even stronger.

Affirmation & Gratitude

I am grateful for love and connection, trusting honesty and vulnerability to strengthen the bonds that matter most.

Capricorn
11 January 2026

Your creativity awakens under today's influence. You may feel pulled toward art, writing, or simply finding beauty in daily routines. Allow yourself to play without demanding perfection. This spark can inspire solutions to practical issues in surprising ways. Don't underestimate the power of joy—it's not frivolous; it's fuel. The cosmos reminds you that life is richer when you balance responsibility with expression. What you create today could ripple into lasting inspiration.

Affirmation & Gratitude

I celebrate my creativity and gratitude for the joy it brings, knowing expression is as vital as responsibility.

Capricorn
12 January 2026

Today highlights your health and well-being. You may be prompted to reconsider your routines—what supports you and what drains you. The stars nudge you to make small, realistic adjustments rather than sweeping, unsustainable changes. Whether it's better sleep, nourishing food, or gentle movement, even one shift can boost your energy. Your body is your foundation, Capricorn—caring for it now ensures you have the stamina to chase the bigger dreams ahead.

Affirmation & Gratitude

I am grateful for my body and honor it with choices that nurture energy, balance, and long-term vitality.

Capricorn
13 January 2026

Your partnerships—personal or professional—are spotlighted again today. Collaboration offers opportunities, but so does learning how to assert your independence gracefully. The stars suggest you may be asked to compromise, but remember compromise doesn't mean sacrifice. Hold to your boundaries while respecting others. Partnerships thrive when both sides feel heard and valued. A meaningful connection today could blossom into a long-term support system, provided you build it on mutual respect and trust.

Affirmation & Gratitude

I am grateful for partnerships that bring balance and growth, knowing healthy connections thrive on respect, trust, and

Capricorn
14 January 2026

The cosmos urges you to look at shared resources—finances, property, or emotional investments with others. Transparency will be vital now. Avoid secrecy or assumptions; clarity prevents conflict later. You may discover hidden strengths in navigating joint ventures or uncover patterns that need adjusting. This isn't about control but about creating fairness and balance. Capricorn, you shine when you ground situations in practicality. Use that gift today to ensure stability for yourself and those you're linked with.

Affirmation & Gratitude

I am grateful for clarity and fairness, trusting that shared resources flow smoothly when built on honesty and respect.

Capricorn
15 January 2026

Capricorn, today draws your focus to broadening horizons. You may feel the urge to learn, teach, or explore new philosophies. Whether through study, travel, or conversation, the stars invite you to step outside your comfort zone. Knowledge you seek now could shape the path ahead in profound ways. Don't dismiss small curiosities—they could plant seeds for future adventures. Remain open and flexible, even if plans don't unfold exactly as expected. Growth thrives when you allow room for discovery.

Affirmation & Gratitude

I am grateful for opportunities to learn and grow, trusting curiosity to lead me to wisdom and expansion.

Capricorn
16 January 2026

Your career sphere is lit today, Capricorn. Authority figures may notice your effort, or you may find yourself leading naturally. With ambition heightened, you could be tempted to push harder than usual. The stars remind you that leadership is about influence, not control. Show others how dedication and patience can yield results without burning out. Recognition is possible now, but staying grounded ensures you don't lose perspective. Let your work speak steadily for itself.

Affirmation & Gratitude

I am grateful for my steady progress, knowing true leadership comes from consistency, humility, and quiet strength.

Capricorn
17 January 2026

Friendships and community take the spotlight today. You may reconnect with old companions or find inspiration through group activities. A sense of belonging fuels your confidence, reminding you that you don't always have to carry everything alone. The stars suggest someone in your circle could present an opportunity or idea that reshapes your future goals. Be open to collaboration—it might bring growth faster than going solo. Nurture your tribe; they nourish you in return.

Affirmation & Gratitude

I am grateful for supportive friendships and communities, trusting shared energy and encouragement help me achieve greater

Capricorn
18 January 2026

Solitude calls today. The cosmos encourages introspection and rest, urging you to step back from the noise. You may feel drawn to meditation, journaling, or simply quiet reflection. The insights you gain now will provide clarity for choices ahead. Don't underestimate the power of stillness—it strengthens your resolve. Emotional healing is possible if you allow yourself to release old burdens. Trust that stepping back today is preparing you for stronger steps tomorrow.

Affirmation & Gratitude

I am grateful for moments of solitude, knowing reflection renews my spirit and reveals the wisdom within.

Capricorn
19 January 2026

Your birthday season begins, Capricorn! The Sun's shift into your sign highlights your identity, purpose, and fresh starts. You're reminded that the year is yours to shape with clarity and intention. The cosmos encourages you to embrace both your strengths and vulnerabilities, knowing they create your true power. A renewed sense of energy fuels your ambitions. Celebrate yourself today, not just for what you've achieved but for who you've become through persistence.

Affirmation & Gratitude

I am grateful for the gift of a new cycle, honoring my strength and embracing new beginnings with courage.

Capricorn
20 January 2026

Today's energy urges you to focus on financial independence and self-worth. You may reconsider how you earn, spend, or invest. The stars highlight the need for balance between security and freedom. Ask yourself: does my money reflect my values? Aligning finances with purpose builds confidence and stability. Small, consistent steps will yield long-term rewards. This is about empowerment, Capricorn—trust your ability to manage resources wisely while also enjoying the fruits of your effort.

Affirmation & Gratitude

I am grateful for financial wisdom and the steady growth it brings, supporting both security and freedom in my life.

Capricorn
21 January 2026

Communication is emphasized now. Conversations may carry more weight than usual, offering opportunities for breakthroughs or misunderstandings depending on how you approach them. The stars encourage honesty with tact—clear words foster stronger bonds. Writing, speaking, or even teaching could come naturally today. Share your perspective with confidence but also remain open to hearing others. Dialogue now has the potential to inspire change or resolve lingering conflicts. Lean into your gift for steady reasoning.

Affirmation & Gratitude

I am grateful for open and clear communication, knowing my words and listening skills create stronger, healthier

Capricorn
22 January 2026

Capricorn, today is about grounding yourself. The stars show a tug-of-war between what you think you should do and what your heart whispers. Practicality usually wins for you, but don't ignore your inner voice. A decision may present itself that seems purely logical, yet intuition is urging you to look deeper. By trusting both reason and instinct, you'll find the path that's steady and aligned. Balance is your secret weapon now—use it wisely.

Affirmation & Gratitude

I am grateful for the balance of logic and intuition, knowing both guide me toward wise, aligned choices.

Capricorn
23 January 2026

The Moon illuminates your home and family life today. Domestic matters may take priority, whether it's repairing something physical or mending emotional bonds. You may feel the need to create a more comfortable, peaceful environment. The stars encourage you to express gratitude for the sanctuary you already have, while making small improvements for the future. Nurturing your personal space now replenishes you, giving you strength for the larger goals you're working toward.

Affirmation & Gratitude

I am grateful for my home and the peace it brings, honoring it as my sanctuary and place of renewal.

Capricorn
24 January 2026

Today brings a focus on creativity and self-expression. You may feel inspired to share ideas or talents you've been holding back. Don't let self-doubt stop you—your unique perspective has value. Whether through writing, conversation, or an artistic outlet, allow yourself to shine without expectation of perfection. The stars highlight the joy that comes from expressing yourself simply because it feels right. Playfulness sparks new insights you can carry into practical endeavors later.

Affirmation & Gratitude

I am grateful for the gift of creativity and embrace my voice with confidence, joy, and authenticity.

Capricorn
25 January 2026

The energy today turns toward work and routines. You may notice inefficiencies in your daily habits or responsibilities and feel called to adjust them. Capricorn, your ability to strategize will help you simplify and streamline. The stars encourage you not to overwhelm yourself with sweeping changes. Instead, small, consistent improvements will bring lasting results. Focus on what truly serves your well-being and discard what drains you unnecessarily. Discipline becomes your ally today.

Affirmation & Gratitude

I am grateful for the structure in my life, and I refine my habits to support growth, balance, and well-being.

Capricorn
26 January 2026

Relationships are in focus, and a key interaction today may teach you something important about compromise and patience. You may feel the urge to prove a point, but the stars remind you that true connection comes from listening as much as speaking. This is an opportunity to strengthen bonds by showing empathy, even if you disagree. Partnerships thrive when respect outweighs pride. Your steady presence can transform tension into cooperation.

Affirmation & Gratitude

I am grateful for the lessons in connection, knowing mutual respect builds relationships that nurture strength, trust, and harmony.

Capricorn
27 January 2026

Shared resources, finances, or emotional investments with others come to the forefront today. A situation may require transparency and courage in addressing boundaries. The stars suggest that fairness and honesty will create solutions where secrecy or control would only create division. You have the ability to ground negotiations and find stability for everyone involved. Trust that by bringing clarity to complex issues, you're not only protecting yourself but also fostering trust in others.

Affirmation & Gratitude

I am grateful for clarity and fairness in shared matters, trusting honesty and balance to build lasting stability.

Capricorn
28 January 2026

Expansion and growth are highlighted today. You may feel called to learn, teach, or pursue an experience that stretches your worldview. The stars encourage you to welcome opportunities that push you outside your usual structures. While change can feel daunting, Capricorn, it's also where growth takes root. Seek wisdom from books, conversations, or even travel if possible. The insight you gain now could inspire long-term direction for your personal or professional journey.

Affirmation & Gratitude

I am grateful for opportunities that broaden my horizons, knowing growth comes from curiosity, courage, and stepping beyond

Capricorn
29 January 2026

Capricorn, today highlights your career and reputation. You may feel pressure to prove yourself, but the stars encourage you to pause and recognize how far you've already come. Recognition is possible, but don't chase it at the expense of your authenticity. Instead, lead by example—steady, consistent effort always speaks louder than showy gestures. A mentor or authority figure may provide guidance now, helping you refine your long-term goals. Remember, your success is not a sprint but a carefully built legacy.

Affirmation & Gratitude

I am grateful for the steady path of success, honoring patience and authenticity as the cornerstones of my legacy.

Capricorn
30 January 2026

Community and friendships are illuminated today. You may feel drawn to reconnect with friends or contribute to a group cause. The stars show that your influence within your network is growing, and collaboration could lead to new opportunities. Don't underestimate the power of shared vision—it can carry you further than going it alone. Capricorn, while independence is your strength, support from others can lighten the load and spark creative solutions. Say yes to connection today.

Affirmation & Gratitude

I am grateful for my supportive circle, knowing shared energy and encouragement make the journey richer and lighter.

Capricorn
31 January 2026

The month closes with a call for introspection and spiritual renewal. The cosmos urges you to slow down, review January's lessons, and realign intentions for the months ahead. Trust that quiet reflection is not wasted time—it's where clarity forms. Dreams, intuition, or subtle signs may hold meaning now, guiding your next steps. Capricorn, honor the balance of achievement and rest. By pausing, you allow the universe to whisper its guidance for February.

Affirmation & Gratitude

I am grateful for moments of reflection, trusting silence and intuition to guide me into the next chapter with clarity.

February 2026

Capricorn
01 February 2026

Capricorn, February begins with a burst of energy around your personal identity. You may feel more self-aware and eager to step into a new version of yourself. The stars encourage you to consider how your daily choices reflect your authentic goals. This is a time for bold self-expression without fear of judgment. Trust your instincts as you put ideas into motion. By owning your story, you give others permission to do the same.

Affirmation & Gratitude

I am grateful for the courage to be fully myself, trusting authenticity to guide me toward meaningful success.

Capricorn
02 February 2026

The cosmos turns your focus to finances and self-worth. A decision about spending, saving, or investing may arise. Capricorn, your natural caution is an asset, but don't let fear of loss stop you from making wise moves. Look for balance—ensuring security while still enjoying life. Today's insights may highlight how your values connect to the way you manage money. Aligning financial choices with your heart will bring both peace and prosperity.

Affirmation & Gratitude

I am grateful for financial wisdom, knowing each choice I make reflects both security and what truly matters to me.

Capricorn
03 February 2026

Communication takes center stage today. Expect conversations that feel important or reveal hidden truths. You may find yourself writing, speaking, or teaching with clarity and influence. However, the stars caution against speaking without considering your words carefully—misunderstandings could arise. Listen as much as you talk; genuine dialogue builds trust. A chance encounter or message could spark ideas for your next steps. Capricorn, your voice carries weight—use it with purpose.

Affirmation & Gratitude

I am grateful for clear and meaningful communication, trusting my words to uplift and connect with others authentically.

Capricorn
04 February 2026

Your home and family life are emphasized. Domestic responsibilities may require attention, or you may simply feel the need to retreat into your sanctuary. The stars suggest strengthening your roots now, whether through physical improvements or healing family bonds. Capricorn, you thrive when your foundation feels stable—today is about creating that comfort. By nurturing your personal space, you recharge your energy for the professional and public demands waiting beyond your doorstep.

Affirmation & Gratitude

I am grateful for the peace of my home, knowing strong roots provide strength for every other part of life.

Capricorn
05 February 2026

Creativity and romance are highlighted today. You may feel a surge of inspiration, or your heart may long for more passion and joy. The cosmos encourages you to engage in something playful or expressive, free from self-criticism. Whether through art, love, or hobbies, allow yourself to experience pleasure. These lighter energies are not distractions—they are nourishment for your spirit. Capricorn, balance seriousness with joy, and your world will feel fuller.

Affirmation & Gratitude

I am grateful for joy and creative sparks, knowing they fuel both my spirit and my practical pursuits.

Capricorn
06 February 2026

The focus turns to health and routines. The stars encourage you to pay attention to your daily habits, especially those impacting energy and well-being. This is not a call for perfection but for awareness. Small, consistent actions will strengthen your body and mind. Capricorn, discipline is your ally—use it to create supportive structures. Trust that by refining your routines, you'll gain the vitality needed to pursue bigger goals with confidence.

Affirmation & Gratitude

I am grateful for the strength my routines provide, honoring small daily steps that create lasting vitality and balance.

Capricorn
07 February 2026

Relationships come into the spotlight. Whether romantic, professional, or social, today offers a chance to deepen bonds. The stars encourage honest dialogue and compromise without losing sight of your needs. Capricorn, your natural steadiness makes you a reliable partner, but remember to allow others space to contribute equally. A moment of vulnerability could open the door to greater trust. Partnership thrives when both people feel valued and respected.

Affirmation & Gratitude

I am grateful for healthy, balanced relationships built on respect, compromise, and the willingness to show both strength and

Capricorn
08 February 2026

Capricorn, today highlights shared resources, both financial and emotional. You may need to navigate boundaries in partnerships or clarify expectations around commitments. Transparency is key—the stars encourage honest discussions rather than avoiding uncomfortable topics. This isn't about control but about fairness and balance. By addressing things openly, you strengthen trust and avoid misunderstandings. Capricorn, your grounded presence helps stabilize these situations. Trust your ability to bring clarity where others feel uncertain.

Affirmation & Gratitude

I am grateful for honesty and fairness in all exchanges, creating stability and trust in both financial and emotional partnerships.

Capricorn
09 February 2026

The stars illuminate your desire for growth and exploration. You may feel pulled toward study, travel, or experiences that broaden your horizons. Opportunities may appear suddenly, so remain flexible. Capricorn, your structured nature sometimes resists the unknown, but today encourages you to take a chance. By stepping outside your usual boundaries, you'll find inspiration that reshapes long-term goals. The universe rewards you courage to expand beyond comfort zones.

Affirmation & Gratitude

I am grateful for new experiences that stretch my perspective, trusting each step into the unknown enriches my life deeply.

Capricorn
10 February 2026

Career matters come into sharp focus today. Recognition for your steady efforts may arrive, or responsibilities may feel heavier than usual. The stars urge you to assess whether your current path reflects your deeper ambitions. Capricorn, leadership comes naturally, but today's energy reminds you that leadership also means guiding with compassion, not just authority. Your patience and discipline are noticed—trust that steady progress brings greater rewards than quick wins.

Affirmation & Gratitude

I am grateful for my resilience and leadership, knowing patience and dedication are the keys to lasting success.

Capricorn
11 February 2026

Friendships and communities are emphasized today. Someone in your circle may inspire a fresh idea or present an unexpected opportunity. The stars remind you that collaboration multiplies possibilities—teamwork often achieves what solo effort cannot. Capricorn, while independence is your strength, don't overlook the value of connection. Lean into group energy, share your wisdom, and be open to learning from others. Together, you'll create momentum for bigger dreams.

Affirmation & Gratitude

I am grateful for my supportive circle, knowing shared vision and teamwork help us all grow stronger and achieve more.

Capricorn
12 February 2026

The cosmos calls for rest and inner reflection today. You may feel drained from constant effort, making solitude essential. Take time to pause, meditate, or journal. The insights you uncover in silence can guide your next steps. Capricorn, you sometimes undervalue rest, but it's the secret fuel for your determination. Today, stillness brings renewal and clarity, preparing you for the challenges ahead. Trust that slowing down creates greater long-term momentum.

Affirmation & Gratitude

I am grateful for quiet moments of renewal, trusting reflection to restore my spirit and strengthen my future steps.

Capricorn
13 February 2026

The Sun highlights your sign today, amplifying your energy and sense of identity. You may feel an urge to assert yourself more strongly or redefine how others see you. Capricorn, embrace this opportunity to show your authentic self without apology. Your confidence inspires those around you. The stars suggest this is an excellent day to set intentions that align with your personal truth. You are stepping into your own authority.

Affirmation & Gratitude

I am grateful for the confidence to be fully myself, shining authentically and embracing the power of self-expression.

Capricorn
14 February 2026

Valentine's Day brings relationships into the spotlight. Whether single or partnered, today emphasizes love, connection, and vulnerability. The stars encourage you to express appreciation openly—love doesn't always require grand gestures; small acts of sincerity matter most. Capricorn, your steadiness makes others feel safe, but showing your softer side deepens intimacy. A heartfelt exchange today could create lasting memories. Celebrate both the love you give and the love you allow yourself to receive.

Affirmation & Gratitude

I am grateful for love in all its forms, embracing both giving and receiving with an open and trusting heart.

Capricorn
15 February 2026

Capricorn, today focuses on finances and self-worth. You may be asked to review spending habits or make decisions about investments. The stars highlight the importance of aligning money with values, not just security. Your natural caution helps, but don't let fear hold you back from opportunities that can grow your resources. By grounding choices in practicality and vision, you strengthen both your confidence and stability. Trust your ability to manage wisely while enjoying life's blessings.

Affirmation & Gratitude

I am grateful for financial wisdom and the stability it brings, allowing me to live securely and meaningfully each day.

Capricorn
16 February 2026

Communication is spotlighted today, Capricorn. Expect important conversations, emails, or messages that could influence your direction. The stars encourage honesty delivered with tact—your words carry weight and can inspire or wound. Listen deeply before responding; genuine dialogue creates breakthroughs. This is also a strong day for writing or sharing your perspective publicly. Your clarity of thought shines brightest when paired with patience. Trust that your voice matters, and use it with intention.

Affirmation & Gratitude

I am grateful for the power of my words, knowing clear and thoughtful communication strengthens trust and connection.

Capricorn
17 February 2026

Your home and family life are emphasized now. A situation may call for patience, compassion, or even practical problem-solving around domestic matters. The stars remind you that your sanctuary is the foundation for everything else. Take time to nurture your space, create comfort, or heal family dynamics. Even small improvements can bring greater peace. Capricorn, you thrive when your base feels stable—tend to it lovingly today to fuel your broader ambitions.

Affirmation & Gratitude

I am grateful for the sanctuary of my home, knowing its strength supports every other area of my life.

Capricorn
18 February 2026

Creative sparks ignite today, and your heart seeks joy. You may feel inspired to pursue a hobby, share your talents, or simply find beauty in small things. The stars emphasize that play and fun are not frivolous—they're essential fuel for your spirit. Allow yourself to explore without judgment, and you may stumble on inspiration that reshapes your work or goals. Capricorn, balance your seriousness with delight, and watch life open more fully.

Affirmation & Gratitude

I am grateful for creativity and joy, embracing moments of lightness as nourishment for my soul and inspiration for my path.

Capricorn
19 February 2026

Health and routines take center stage. The cosmos urges you to assess habits that either support or undermine your energy. Even one small change—a walk, better sleep, or mindful eating—can have lasting effects. Capricorn, your discipline allows you to commit to gradual improvements that build resilience. Don't aim for perfection; consistency matters more. When you nurture your body, mind, and spirit, you strengthen the foundation needed to pursue ambitious dreams.

Affirmation & Gratitude

I am grateful for the routines that support my well-being, honoring small steps that create lasting strength and vitality.

Capricorn
20 February 2026

Relationships are spotlighted today. You may need to navigate compromise or find balance between your needs and someone else's. The stars encourage you to approach discussions with empathy, ensuring both voices are heard. Healthy partnerships are built on trust and mutual respect. Capricorn, while your steadiness makes you reliable, remember to also allow vulnerability. By opening yourself to others, you deepen bonds and create more harmonious connections.

Affirmation & Gratitude

I am grateful for balanced relationships, built on mutual respect, understanding, and the courage to show both strength and

Capricorn
21 February 2026

Shared resources and emotional investments rise to the surface. Issues around trust, finances, or power dynamics may need clarity. The stars urge transparency—avoiding difficult conversations only creates tension later. Capricorn, your practicality equips you to ground these matters with fairness. Trust yourself to set healthy boundaries while also honoring commitments. By facing things directly, you turn potential conflicts into opportunities for deeper trust and stability. This courage strengthens both you and your connections.

Affirmation & Gratitude

I am grateful for honesty and fairness in shared matters, trusting courage and clarity to create security for all involved.

Capricorn
22 February 2026

Capricorn, today invites you to expand your horizons. You may feel a restless urge to explore, whether through learning, travel, or fresh ideas. The stars encourage you to seek wisdom outside your usual routines. This doesn't have to be dramatic—even a new book, conversation, or practice can shift your perspective. Growth now comes from being willing to step beyond comfort zones. Your grounded nature ensures that these explorations become more than fleeting experiences—they become lasting insights.

Affirmation & Gratitude
I am grateful for opportunities that expand my mind and spirit, welcoming growth that shapes my journey with wisdom and courage.

Capricorn
23 February 2026

Career and public image come into focus today. You may be recognized for past efforts or asked to step into greater responsibility. The stars highlight your leadership qualities—others naturally look to you for guidance. Yet remember: true leadership is about presence, not pressure. Stay humble, Capricorn, while still owning your authority. Decisions made today could ripple into long-term progress. Trust that your patience and dedication will carve the reputation you've worked so hard to build.

Affirmation & Gratitude

I am grateful for my steady progress, knowing my dedication and patience create a lasting legacy of success and respect.

Capricorn
24 February 2026

The cosmos highlights your friendships and networks. You may reconnect with someone important, or find inspiration within your social circles. Group projects or community involvement could flourish today. Capricorn, while independence defines you, remember that collaboration multiplies potential. Sharing ideas now may spark opportunities you wouldn't discover alone. Stay open to advice or encouragement offered by others—sometimes support arrives from unexpected places. Your connections today remind you of the power of collective energy.

Affirmation & Gratitude

I am grateful for supportive friendships and communities, knowing shared vision and teamwork create growth and joy beyond what

Capricorn
25 February 2026

Rest and introspection take priority. You may feel drained or contemplative, as though the universe is nudging you to pause. The stars suggest that quiet reflection today will reveal insights you've been too busy to notice. Capricorn, you sometimes equate productivity with worth, but rest is essential for clarity. Journaling, meditation, or even a simple walk can bring perspective. Trust that stillness now creates the strength you'll need for what comes next.

Affirmation & Gratitude

I am grateful for the gift of rest and reflection, knowing quiet moments restore my spirit and reveal inner guidance.

Capricorn
26 February 2026

The Sun lights up your identity and self-expression. You may feel stronger in asserting who you are and what you stand for. Capricorn, embrace your authentic self unapologetically. The stars suggest this is a day for bold choices—ones that reflect your truth rather than expectations. Your presence is magnetic now, so step forward with confidence. By honoring yourself, you also inspire others to embrace their own authenticity.

Affirmation & Gratitude
I am grateful for the strength to stand in my truth, embracing authenticity as the foundation of my confidence and joy.

Capricorn
27 February 2026

The focus turns to finances and self-worth again. You may review your resources, budget, or values, realizing adjustments are needed. The stars encourage practical steps: create structure where money feels uncertain, and remind yourself of your worth beyond material security. Capricorn, stability is important, but so is recognizing abundance in non-material forms. Today is about strengthening both financial and emotional foundations, ensuring they align with your larger goals.

Affirmation & Gratitude

I am grateful for the balance of financial stability and inner worth, trusting abundance flows in many meaningful forms.

Capricorn
28 February 2026

February closes with a surge of communication. Conversations may carry importance, or you may feel compelled to share your thoughts more openly. The stars encourage clarity and honesty—your words have influence now. Writing, teaching, or even casual exchanges could spark significant opportunities. Capricorn, your grounded voice can guide others while also opening doors for yourself. Don't hold back from speaking your truth today—it may be exactly what someone needs to hear.

Affirmation & Gratitude

I am grateful for the clarity and strength of my voice, trusting communication to connect me with opportunities and growth.

March
2026

Capricorn
01 March 2026

Capricorn, the month opens with an emphasis on home, family, and your emotional foundation. You may feel called to nurture your living space or reconnect with loved ones. The stars encourage you to invest time into creating harmony within your personal sanctuary. Even small adjustments—decluttering, cooking a meal, or sharing heartfelt words—bring warmth and balance. Remember, your outer ambitions are stronger when your inner world feels secure. Home is not just where you live; it's where your spirit finds rest.

Affirmation & Gratitude

I am grateful for the stability of my home and family, knowing peace within creates strength for everything outside.

Capricorn
02 March 2026

Creativity and joy come alive today. You may feel inspired to try something playful or to express your talents more boldly. The cosmos reminds you that fun is not a distraction but a source of renewal. Capricorn, you sometimes view leisure as secondary to duty, yet joy fuels your productivity. Whether through art, romance, or laughter, embrace the lighter side of life. What you create or feel today could spark long-lasting motivation.

Affirmation & Gratitude

I am grateful for joy and creativity, trusting play and expression to fuel my heart and energize my ambitions.

Capricorn
03 March 2026

Work, health, and routines are in focus. You may notice inefficiencies or unhealthy habits that drain your energy. The stars encourage you to refine, not overhaul, your daily systems. Capricorn, your discipline makes you excellent at building sustainable habits, so lean into that strength. Even a small change—more water, better sleep, or a clearer schedule—will ripple forward. Today is about practical steps that ensure long-term resilience and well-being.

Affirmation & Gratitude

I am grateful for supportive routines that nourish my body and mind, creating balance, strength, and consistency each day.

Capricorn
04 March 2026

Relationships take center stage today. The stars highlight the importance of cooperation and empathy. You may feel tested in a partnership, asked to compromise or show patience. Remember, Capricorn, strength in relationships comes from balance—honoring your needs while respecting others. Vulnerability is not weakness; it's how trust deepens. A key conversation today could resolve misunderstandings and bring greater closeness. Your steady energy is a gift—share it with those who matter.

Affirmation & Gratitude

I am grateful for the love and respect in my relationships, knowing balance and openness strengthen every bond I cherish.

Capricorn
05 March 2026

Shared resources, joint ventures, or emotional investments demand your attention today. A financial matter may surface, or you may be asked to address trust and boundaries with someone close. The cosmos encourages openness—avoid secrecy or assumptions. Capricorn, your practical nature helps you navigate this terrain with fairness. By seeking clarity, you create stability for yourself and others. This is not about control but about ensuring balance and mutual respect in shared commitments.

Affirmation & Gratitude

I am grateful for honesty and fairness in all shared matters, knowing transparency creates trust, stability, and mutual respect.

Capricorn
06 March 2026

Growth and exploration are highlighted. You may feel inspired to learn, travel, or connect with new philosophies. The stars encourage you to step beyond comfort zones, even in small ways. Capricorn, your grounded nature ensures that whatever you pursue will be integrated meaningfully. This is an excellent day to expand your perspective, embrace curiosity, and consider how new insights align with your long-term vision. Every step toward knowledge enriches your journey.

Affirmation & Gratitude

I am grateful for opportunities that expand my horizons, trusting curiosity and learning to guide me toward greater wisdom.

Capricorn
07 March 2026

Your career and reputation shine under today's sky. Recognition for your hard work may arrive, or you may feel motivated to plan long-term ambitions. The stars remind you to lead with both confidence and humility—your consistency sets you apart. A mentor figure may appear, offering guidance, or you may inspire others by your steady example. Capricorn, this is a day to step into authority with grace, knowing your dedication is your greatest strength.

Affirmation & Gratitude

I am grateful for my steady progress and leadership, trusting that my efforts create meaningful and lasting success.

Capricorn
08 March 2026

Capricorn, friendships and networks are highlighted today. You may reconnect with someone who inspires you or discover an opportunity through your community. The stars encourage collaboration—your ideas gain momentum when combined with others. Don't underestimate casual conversations; they may hold seeds for future growth. Remember, while independence defines you, support strengthens you. Trust the connections you've built and lean on them now. By engaging with your circle, you'll find both encouragement and inspiration.

Affirmation & Gratitude

I am grateful for my circle of friends and allies, knowing shared energy and vision create powerful momentum forward.

Capricorn
09 March 2026

The cosmos calls you inward today. Rest, solitude, and reflection bring clarity you can't find in constant motion. Dreams or intuitive nudges may carry important messages, so pay attention to subtle cues. Capricorn, you often equate progress with external results, but true strength comes from inner alignment. Today, slowing down is not weakness—it's wisdom. By pausing, you gather insight to make stronger choices when the pace quickens again.

Affirmation & Gratitude

I am grateful for moments of quiet and stillness, trusting reflection to guide me toward wisdom and peace.

Capricorn
10 March 2026

The Sun highlights your sense of identity and self-expression. You may feel a renewed drive to assert yourself or pursue personal goals. Capricorn, step forward confidently, but ensure your actions align with your true values. Authenticity now attracts the right opportunities and people to you. The stars remind you that shining your light doesn't diminish others—it inspires them. Today is a day to stand tall and own your presence fully.

Affirmation & Gratitude

I am grateful for the courage to be authentically me, shining my light with confidence and integrity.

Capricorn
11 March 2026

Finances and self-worth take center stage. You may review budgets, consider new income streams, or reassess spending habits. The stars encourage practicality without fear—abundance grows when money aligns with values. Capricorn, you're skilled at building steady foundations, so trust your instincts while staying open to fresh ideas. Your relationship with money mirrors your relationship with self-worth; strengthen one, and the other follows. Today is about security, empowerment, and purposeful choices.

Affirmation & Gratitude

I am grateful for financial wisdom and self-worth, knowing alignment brings both abundance and confidence into my life.

Capricorn
12 March 2026

Communication flows strongly today. Conversations may bring clarity, or you may feel compelled to share ideas more openly. The cosmos encourages you to use your words carefully—your voice holds weight and influence. Writing, teaching, or public speaking could be particularly fruitful. Capricorn, your steady reasoning can calm others and guide them toward solutions. Stay open to listening, too—important insights may come from unexpected sources. Dialogue today creates bridges where gaps once stood.

Affirmation & Gratitude

I am grateful for meaningful conversations, trusting clear and honest communication to build trust and connection.

Capricorn
13 March 2026

Your home and family life are emphasized. You may feel a pull toward strengthening your sanctuary, whether by practical tasks or emotional healing. Capricorn, your drive often keeps you focused outward, but today the stars urge you to tend to your inner world. Creating peace in your environment allows you to recharge and pursue ambitions with renewed strength. Nurture both your space and the relationships that matter most.

Affirmation & Gratitude

I am grateful for the sanctuary of my home, knowing peace here fuels strength for all I do beyond it.

Capricorn
14 March 2026

Joy, romance, and creativity light up today's sky. You may feel playful, inspired, or drawn to connect with your passions. The stars remind you that fun is not indulgence—it's essential fuel for your spirit. Capricorn, allow yourself to break routine and embrace beauty. Expressing yourself without expectation brings freedom. Whether in love, art, or laughter, lean into what makes you feel alive. Today, delight carries wisdom and renewal.

Affirmation & Gratitude

I am grateful for joy, love, and creativity, embracing the lightness that nourishes my spirit and uplifts my heart.

Capricorn
15 March 2026

Capricorn, today highlights work, health, and routines. You may feel called to reorganize your schedule, refine habits, or tackle tasks you've been avoiding. The stars encourage a practical yet gentle approach—progress comes from consistency, not perfection. A small shift today, like clearer boundaries around your time or more mindful meals, can ripple into lasting benefits. Capricorn, your discipline is powerful, but allow room for flexibility too. Balance ensures sustainability. Today is about building foundations for resilience, not exhausting yourself with over-effort.

Affirmation & Gratitude

I am grateful for supportive habits, trusting steady improvements create lasting balance, health, and strength in my life.

Capricorn
16 March 2026

Relationships are emphasized now. You may find yourself negotiating, compromising, or deepening bonds with a partner, colleague, or friend. The stars encourage honest communication, reminding you that partnerships thrive on both give and take. Capricorn, your steadiness offers reassurance, but don't be afraid to reveal vulnerability—it creates deeper trust. Today's interactions may highlight where balance is lacking. By addressing issues openly, you build stronger, healthier connections that support your long-term growth and happiness.

Affirmation & Gratitude

I am grateful for balanced and respectful relationships, where trust, honesty, and care create harmony and strength.

Capricorn
17 March 2026

Shared resources, finances, or emotional investments may surface today. You may need to clarify agreements or reassess boundaries with others. The stars urge fairness—avoid clinging too tightly or letting resentment fester. Transparency strengthens trust. Capricorn, your practical wisdom allows you to stabilize situations that might otherwise feel uncertain. By facing matters directly, you prevent small misunderstandings from becoming larger conflicts. Today's courage to confront the truth will bring long-term security for everyone involved.

Affirmation & Gratitude

I am grateful for clarity and fairness in shared matters, trusting honesty builds trust and stability in all partnerships.

Capricorn
18 March 2026

Exploration and growth call to you today. You may crave new experiences—learning, travel, or broadening your perspective through fresh ideas. The stars encourage you to step outside routine and embrace curiosity. Capricorn, your grounded approach ensures these adventures have lasting impact rather than being fleeting whims. Opportunities may appear suddenly, so stay open and flexible. Today is about expanding your mind and spirit, finding meaning beyond the practical. Adventure holds wisdom—trust its call.

Affirmation & Gratitude

I am grateful for opportunities to expand my perspective, welcoming growth and wisdom that enrich my journey.

Capricorn
19 March 2026

Career and reputation are in the spotlight. Recognition for your efforts may arrive, or responsibilities could feel heavier than usual. The stars remind you that patience and persistence are your allies—success is rarely instant. Capricorn, lead with integrity, and your reputation will speak for itself. Someone in authority may take notice, opening doors to future opportunities. Stay grounded, knowing your steady contributions build a legacy stronger than any quick achievement.

Affirmation & Gratitude

I am grateful for recognition of my steady efforts, trusting patience and persistence create meaningful, lasting success.

Capricorn
20 March 2026

Friendships and community connections brighten your day. Someone in your circle may inspire a new idea or extend a helping hand. The stars encourage you to nurture your network—collaboration will carry you further than working alone. Capricorn, while independence is your strength, remember that allies provide support and motivation. Today is about shared goals, laughter, and encouragement. Treasure the bonds that uplift you; they're part of your foundation for success and joy.

Affirmation & Gratitude

I am grateful for my community, knowing shared vision and support strengthen and uplift me.

Capricorn
21 March 2026

Solitude and reflection become essential today. The cosmos asks you to pause, rest, and realign. Capricorn, you often prioritize productivity, but inner renewal is equally important. Dreams or intuition may offer guidance, so listen carefully to subtle messages. This quiet space allows you to release burdens and gather clarity for the next chapter. Stillness today is not wasted—it's fuel for the strength you'll need tomorrow.

Affirmation & Gratitude

I am grateful for peaceful moments of reflection, trusting rest restores my clarity and strengthens my spirit.

Capricorn
22 March 2026

Capricorn, today shines a light on your sense of self and personal expression. You may feel stronger in asserting your individuality or showcasing talents that have been under wraps. The stars encourage you to step into the spotlight with confidence, without fear of judgment. Authenticity attracts the right opportunities and connections. By owning who you are, you remind others they too can live truthfully. Today's courage sets a tone for months ahead.

Affirmation & Gratitude

I am grateful for the confidence to live authentically, knowing my truth inspires both myself and others.

Capricorn
23 March 2026

Finances and self-worth are emphasized. You may review spending, income, or the value you place on your skills. The cosmos encourages you to connect money with meaning, ensuring your resources support not just survival but fulfillment. Capricorn, you're excellent at building security, but remember abundance also includes gratitude and joy. By aligning financial choices with values, you create both stability and purpose. A small step toward financial clarity today yields lasting peace.

Affirmation & Gratitude

I am grateful for financial stability and self-worth, trusting my choices reflect both security and purpose.

Capricorn
24 March 2026

Conversations carry weight today. The stars encourage you to share your thoughts honestly while also listening to others' perspectives. Misunderstandings may arise if you rush, but patience and clarity resolve them quickly. Capricorn, your words hold influence—use them thoughtfully. This is a favorable day for writing, teaching, or making an important call. Speak from both mind and heart; your ability to balance reason with empathy will win trust and open doors.

Affirmation & Gratitude

I am grateful for meaningful dialogue, trusting my words to create clarity and deeper connections.

Capricorn
25 March 2026

Your home and family sphere comes into focus. Domestic matters may require your attention, whether it's caring for loved ones or refreshing your living space. The stars remind you that tending to your personal sanctuary supports your outer ambitions. Capricorn, balance is key—creating harmony at home allows you to pursue career and public goals with greater strength. Small acts of nurturing now ripple into long-term stability and peace for your household.

Affirmation & Gratitude

I am grateful for the peace and strength my home provides, knowing it fuels every part of my journey.

Capricorn
26 March 2026

Creativity, romance, and playfulness fill the air. You may feel inspired to dive into a hobby, express yourself artistically, or simply laugh more freely. The cosmos reminds you that joy is not frivolous—it's nourishment. Capricorn, responsibilities can weigh heavily, but balance comes when you allow fun to restore your spirit. Expressing your heart without judgment today sparks inspiration that flows into other areas of your life.

Affirmation & Gratitude

I am grateful for joy and creativity, embracing lighthearted moments as fuel for my soul and strength for my path.

Capricorn
27 March 2026

Work, health, and routines take center stage. You may notice areas of inefficiency or habits that drain your energy. The stars encourage small adjustments rather than drastic changes. Capricorn, your discipline makes you excellent at building supportive structures—lean into that strength today. By focusing on practical improvements, you lay the groundwork for sustainable success. Remember, your health and energy are your greatest assets—protect them with mindful daily choices.

Affirmation & Gratitude

I am grateful for healthy routines that support my well-being, trusting consistency builds resilience and strength.

Capricorn
28 March 2026

Relationships are emphasized today. The cosmos suggests a situation may call for compromise, patience, or deeper understanding. Capricorn, your natural steadiness provides security in partnerships, but remember to also allow space for vulnerability and emotional expression. Healthy bonds thrive on both strength and softness. A heartfelt conversation today could resolve tension or bring you closer together. By approaching connections with openness, you build harmony and trust that lasts.

Affirmation & Gratitude

I am grateful for love and respect in my relationships, knowing openness and care strengthen every bond.

Capricorn
29 March 2026

Capricorn, shared resources and deeper emotional investments come into the spotlight today. You may need to address financial arrangements, boundaries, or issues of trust in partnerships. The stars encourage you to be transparent and practical—avoid letting assumptions or fears complicate matters. Your grounded nature gives you the ability to stabilize these conversations with fairness. By facing situations directly, you create security for yourself and others. Trust that honesty and clarity are the building blocks of lasting connection.

Affirmation & Gratitude

I am grateful for the courage to address shared matters with honesty, creating fairness, stability, and trust in all connections.

Capricorn
30 March 2026

The cosmos encourages growth and expansion today. You may feel restless for new experiences, learning opportunities, or travel. Capricorn, while you often prioritize structure, today is about breaking routine and broadening your horizons. Inspiration may come from a conversation, a book, or an unexpected opportunity. Don't dismiss curiosity—it's the spark that leads to meaningful transformation. By embracing new perspectives, you'll find greater wisdom that enriches both your personal and professional path.

Affirmation & Gratitude

I am grateful for opportunities to explore and grow, trusting curiosity to lead me toward wisdom and fulfillment.

Capricorn
31 March 2026

Your career and public reputation are illuminated today. Recognition for your steady efforts may arrive, or you may be asked to shoulder new responsibilities. Capricorn, the stars remind you to lead with humility as well as authority. Your persistence sets you apart, and others notice your reliability. Use today to refine long-term goals, ensuring they align with both ambition and authenticity. Legacy is built step by step —trust the process.

Affirmation & Gratitude

I am grateful for recognition of my steady efforts, trusting my persistence and integrity to create meaningful, lasting success.

April
2026

Capricorn
01 April 2026

Capricorn, April begins with an emphasis on friendships and networks. Someone in your circle may offer fresh ideas or an unexpected opportunity. The stars encourage you to lean into collaboration instead of trying to carry everything alone. By sharing resources and wisdom, you'll find momentum that might not be possible on your own. Capricorn, your independence is admirable, but true strength also comes from community. Today, connection fuels both your spirit and your ambitions.

Affirmation & Gratitude

I am grateful for my community, trusting shared vision and energy to open new opportunities and strengthen my path.

Capricorn
02 April 2026

The cosmos calls for rest and reflection today. You may feel the need to slow down and recharge. Capricorn, silence and solitude bring you insights that constant motion cannot. Trust your dreams, intuition, and subtle signs—they may hold answers to questions you've been carrying. The stars remind you that inner alignment creates outer strength. By pausing now, you gather clarity and energy that will fuel the busy days ahead. Stillness is wisdom.

Affirmation & Gratitude

I am grateful for moments of quiet reflection, trusting rest and intuition to renew my strength and guide my steps.

Capricorn
03 April 2026

The Sun highlights your sense of identity and expression. You may feel stronger in asserting yourself or sharing your talents. Capricorn, today is about showing the world who you really are, without apology. Authenticity attracts genuine opportunities and people. The stars encourage you to trust your voice—it's steady, practical, and inspiring. When you stand tall in your truth, you naturally become a guiding example for others. Shine without fear today.

Affirmation & Gratitude

I am grateful for the confidence to live authentically, trusting my truth to guide me and inspire others.

Capricorn
04 April 2026

Finances and self-worth take the spotlight. You may feel called to reassess your relationship with money or your values. Capricorn, you're naturally cautious, but the stars encourage you to also consider how your resources support fulfillment, not just security. Aligning money with meaning ensures both prosperity and peace of mind. Remember, your worth is not tied solely to material success—it's also reflected in the richness of your inner life.

Affirmation & Gratitude

I am grateful for financial stability and self-worth, trusting abundance flows when my values and choices align with my true

Capricorn
05 April 2026

Communication is emphasized today. Important conversations may arise, or you may feel the urge to share your thoughts more openly. Capricorn, your words hold weight—use them carefully and with intention. The stars encourage you to balance logic with empathy, ensuring others feel heard. Writing, teaching, or simply speaking from the heart may carry greater impact than you expect. Stay open to listening too—insight may come from unexpected sources.

Affirmation & Gratitude

I am grateful for the clarity and strength of my words, knowing communication builds trust and opens new opportunities.

Capricorn
06 April 2026

Home and family matters come into focus. You may feel pulled to nurture your space or resolve issues with loved ones. The cosmos encourages you to create harmony within your sanctuary, knowing it supports your broader goals. Capricorn, your ambitions thrive when your foundation feels steady. Small acts of care—repairing, cleaning, or connecting emotionally—create peace and comfort. By tending to your roots today, you fortify the branches of your future growth.

Affirmation & Gratitude

I am grateful for the peace of my home and family, knowing strong roots support everything I build beyond them.

Capricorn
07 April 2026

Joy, romance, and creativity light up your day. You may feel drawn toward hobbies, playful activities, or heartfelt connections. The stars remind you that joy is fuel for your spirit, not a distraction. Capricorn, you often prioritize responsibility, but today, laughter and love are your medicine. Express yourself freely—through art, affection, or simply savoring small moments. What lifts your heart today will inspire resilience in the days to come.

Affirmation & Gratitude

I am grateful for moments of joy and creativity, trusting lightheartedness strengthens my spirit and energizes my path.

Capricorn
08 April 2026

Capricorn, today shines a light on your work, health, and daily routines. You may notice habits that no longer serve you, or tasks that could be streamlined. The stars encourage steady adjustments instead of drastic overhauls. Remember, consistency creates results. Capricorn, your discipline makes you a master of building sustainable structures. Focus on what brings balance between productivity and self-care. Today is about refining your systems so you feel stronger, healthier, and more supported long term.

Affirmation & Gratitude

I am grateful for supportive routines, trusting small and steady changes to create long-lasting strength and balance in my life.

Capricorn
09 April 2026

Partnerships take center stage. You may be called to compromise, negotiate, or lean into cooperation. Capricorn, your steadiness makes you a reliable partner, but remember that relationships thrive when both sides feel valued. The stars encourage openness—allow others to contribute their perspective while you hold space with patience. Vulnerability may feel uncomfortable, yet it strengthens trust. Today, focus on building harmony in your bonds by balancing strength with softness.

Affirmation & Gratitude

I am grateful for the love and respect in my partnerships, knowing balance and openness build lasting connection.

Capricorn
10 April 2026

The cosmos highlights shared resources, joint ventures, or emotional commitments. You may need to clarify agreements, whether financial or personal. Capricorn, your grounded approach helps you manage delicate situations with fairness. The stars encourage transparency—secrets or avoidance only complicate matters. By addressing things directly, you create stability and security for everyone involved. This is a day to honor boundaries while also fostering trust. The courage you show today strengthens future bonds.

Affirmation & Gratitude

I am grateful for honesty and fairness in shared matters, trusting clarity creates harmony and lasting trust.

Capricorn
11 April 2026

Today emphasizes growth, exploration, and broadening horizons. You may feel called to learn, travel, or immerse yourself in new ideas. Capricorn, while you value stability, stepping outside routine now enriches your vision. The stars remind you that curiosity is a powerful teacher. Even a small adventure—like a fresh perspective or new practice—can inspire long-term direction. Open yourself to the world's wisdom, and you'll carry its lessons into future achievements.

Affirmation & Gratitude

I am grateful for opportunities to expand my horizons, knowing curiosity leads me toward wisdom and growth.

Capricorn
12 April 2026

Career and reputation come into focus. Recognition for your steady work may surface, or new responsibilities could arise. Capricorn, your leadership is noticed, but the stars remind you that true influence is earned through consistency and integrity. Today is an excellent time to refine long-term goals, ensuring they align with your deeper purpose. Lead with humility, and you'll gain respect that lasts longer than applause. Your persistence continues to build your legacy.

Affirmation & Gratitude

I am grateful for recognition of my efforts, trusting integrity and patience to create a legacy of meaningful success.

Capricorn
13 April 2026

Friendships and networks are highlighted today. The cosmos encourages collaboration and connection. Someone in your circle may offer inspiration or practical help. Capricorn, your independence is admirable, but community multiplies possibilities. Lean into group energy, share your wisdom, and be open to advice. Today's connections may spark opportunities you couldn't find alone. Cherish the bonds that uplift you; they're part of your foundation for success and fulfillment.

Affirmation & Gratitude

I am grateful for supportive friendships and communities, knowing shared energy and encouragement create stronger paths

Capricorn
14 April 2026

Rest and reflection are vital today. The stars remind you that silence restores what constant effort cannot. Capricorn, you may feel drained, but slowing down allows insight and healing. Pay attention to your dreams and intuition; subtle messages may guide your next steps. Today isn't about pushing forward —it's about pausing so you can continue with clarity and strength. Rest is not wasted—it is preparation for renewal.

Affirmation & Gratitude

I am grateful for peaceful moments of rest, trusting reflection restores my spirit and clarifies my direction.

Capricorn
15 April 2026

Capricorn, the Sun highlights your individuality today, urging you to express your authentic self more boldly. You may feel called to showcase talents, speak your truth, or stand firm in your values. The stars remind you that authenticity attracts genuine opportunities, while compromise for approval only drains you. Capricorn, your steady presence is powerful; when you align with your truth, you naturally inspire others. Today, own your story unapologetically and let it guide your next steps.

Affirmation & Gratitude

I am grateful for the courage to live authentically, trusting my truth attracts the right people and opportunities.

Capricorn
16 April 2026

Finances and self-worth rise to the surface. You may feel prompted to reassess your budget, earning potential, or relationship with money. The stars encourage balance—focus on security without becoming overly rigid. Capricorn, you're gifted at building strong foundations, but remember abundance is also about gratitude and enjoyment. Aligning financial decisions with your deeper values ensures lasting stability. A wise choice today can strengthen both your confidence and your future prosperity.

Affirmation & Gratitude

I am grateful for financial wisdom and self-worth, trusting aligned choices bring security and fulfillment.

Capricorn
17 April 2026

Communication is highlighted today. Conversations may hold more significance than usual, offering chances for breakthroughs or clarity. Capricorn, your words carry weight—choose them with care. The stars remind you that listening is as important as speaking. By balancing reason with empathy, you foster stronger understanding. Today is also excellent for writing, teaching, or sharing your perspective publicly. Don't underestimate the influence of your steady, thoughtful voice. It may reach further than expected.

Affirmation & Gratitude

I am grateful for clear and thoughtful communication, trusting my words and listening skills build meaningful connections.

Capricorn
18 April 2026

Home and family matters take priority. You may feel drawn to nurture your personal sanctuary or resolve family dynamics. The stars encourage you to focus on creating peace and stability within your domestic world. Capricorn, your ambitions soar higher when your roots feel strong. Whether it's practical improvements or emotional healing, tending to your home now strengthens every other area of life. Today is about grounding yourself where it matters most.

Affirmation & Gratitude

I am grateful for the peace of my home and family, knowing harmony here supports all that I build.

Capricorn
19 April 2026

Creativity and joy are illuminated today. You may feel inspired to explore a hobby, express your talents, or embrace romance. The stars remind you that fun is nourishment, not distraction. Capricorn, you often prioritize duty, but today encourages you to celebrate the lighter side of life. By leaning into joy, you replenish energy and spark ideas that may fuel future goals. Today, playfulness carries wisdom.

Affirmation & Gratitude

I am grateful for joy and creativity, embracing play as nourishment for my spirit and inspiration for my journey.

Capricorn
20 April 2026

Work and routines come under review. You may feel called to refine your schedule, adjust habits, or tackle lingering responsibilities. Capricorn, your discipline makes you excellent at building consistency, but don't fall into rigidity. The stars encourage small, supportive changes that prioritize health and balance. By focusing on sustainability rather than perfection, you create routines that carry you forward. Today, efficiency and well-being are your best allies.

Affirmation & Gratitude

I am grateful for healthy, supportive routines that bring structure, balance, and strength to my days.

Capricorn
21 April 2026

Partnerships are emphasized. You may be called to compromise, cooperate, or deepen understanding with someone important. The stars remind you that healthy relationships thrive on trust, empathy, and balance. Capricorn, your steadiness offers stability, but showing vulnerability also strengthens bonds. Today is a chance to build harmony by ensuring both voices are respected. A heartfelt conversation may resolve tension or spark greater closeness.

Affirmation & Gratitude

I am grateful for love and respect in my partnerships, trusting openness and empathy create harmony.

Capricorn
22 April 2026

Capricorn, shared resources and deeper emotional bonds are spotlighted today. You may need to address finances, responsibilities, or trust issues within partnerships. The stars encourage transparency and fairness—avoid assumptions or secrecy. Your natural steadiness helps create balance, ensuring security for both you and others. This is also a powerful day for emotional healing; facing fears directly brings strength. Capricorn, by approaching matters with clarity and courage, you transform tension into stability and deeper trust.

Affirmation & Gratitude

I am grateful for clarity and honesty in shared matters, trusting fairness builds stronger, lasting bonds.

Capricorn
23 April 2026

The cosmos highlights growth and exploration. You may feel a pull toward new knowledge, spiritual practices, or opportunities that broaden your worldview. Capricorn, while you value routine, today reminds you that stepping outside your comfort zone enriches your path. Even small acts—reading a new perspective or speaking with someone different—can spark inspiration. The stars encourage you to welcome change with curiosity rather than resistance. Expansion fuels your wisdom and aligns you with bigger dreams.

Affirmation & Gratitude

I am grateful for opportunities that expand my perspective, welcoming growth with curiosity and courage.

Capricorn
24 April 2026

Career and reputation take the spotlight today. Recognition for your hard work may arrive, or new responsibilities could present themselves. The stars encourage you to embrace leadership with humility and confidence. Capricorn, your persistence is admired, and others notice your reliability. Today is a good time to refine long-term goals, ensuring they align with your deeper purpose. Remember, true success isn't only about achievement—it's also about integrity and the legacy you're building.

Affirmation & Gratitude

I am grateful for recognition of my dedication, trusting patience and integrity to create meaningful success.

Capricorn
25 April 2026

Friendships and communities are emphasized. The stars encourage you to engage with your social circle or contribute to a group project. Capricorn, independence is one of your strengths, but collaboration today brings unexpected opportunities. A conversation with a friend could plant seeds for future ventures. Remember, your network is a source of both support and inspiration. Lean into shared vision; it multiplies your potential beyond what you could achieve alone.

Affirmation & Gratitude

I am grateful for my friendships and communities, trusting shared energy inspires growth and joy.

Capricorn
26 April 2026

Rest and solitude become essential today. The cosmos urges you to step back, recharge, and reflect on recent events. Capricorn, you often equate progress with constant effort, but stillness is equally powerful. Intuition or dreams may offer guidance now—pay attention to subtle messages. By taking time to pause, you prepare yourself for renewed focus and energy in the days ahead. Rest is not a setback—it's preparation for success.

Affirmation & Gratitude

I am grateful for the healing power of rest, trusting reflection restores clarity and strength.

Capricorn
27 April 2026

The Sun lights up your identity and self-expression. You may feel inspired to assert yourself more boldly or show talents you've kept quiet. Capricorn, the stars remind you that authenticity is your greatest strength. By living your truth unapologetically, you attract the right people and opportunities. This is not about being loud; it's about being real. Today, your confidence inspires others to embrace their own authenticity too.

Affirmation & Gratitude

I am grateful for the confidence to shine authentically, trusting my truth attracts aligned opportunities.

Capricorn
28 April 2026

Finances and self-worth rise to the surface again. You may be prompted to reassess your relationship with money, values, or possessions. The stars encourage balance between saving and enjoying life. Capricorn, stability is important, but abundance also means appreciating what you already have. Today is about aligning financial decisions with purpose, ensuring resources support not only security but also fulfillment. When money mirrors values, prosperity flows more meaningfully.

Affirmation & Gratitude

I am grateful for the wisdom to align money with values, creating both security and fulfillment.

Capricorn
29 April 2026

Capricorn, communication is in focus today. You may find yourself in meaningful conversations, whether at work, with friends, or family. The stars encourage clarity and honesty—your words have the power to inspire or heal. Be mindful of tone; patience creates understanding where tension could otherwise build. Writing, teaching, or even sharing your perspective casually could spark unexpected opportunities. Capricorn, your voice is grounded and influential—trust it. Today, dialogue becomes a bridge toward connection and progress.

Affirmation & Gratitude

I am grateful for the clarity and influence of my words, trusting communication builds stronger connections and opportunities.

Capricorn
30 April 2026

Home and family matters are emphasized as April closes. You may feel called to nurture your personal sanctuary or resolve dynamics with loved ones. The stars encourage balance—your ambitions soar higher when your roots feel secure. Even small actions, like tidying your space or spending quality time, create harmony. Capricorn, remember that peace at home provides strength for every other area of life. Today, tend to your foundation with care.

Affirmation & Gratitude

I am grateful for the peace and strength of my home, knowing stability here supports all of my ambitions.

May 2026

Capricorn
01 May 2026

Capricorn, May begins with a spark of creativity and joy. The stars encourage you to embrace hobbies, romance, or playful activities that lift your spirit. Responsibilities often weigh heavily on your shoulders, but today's energy reminds you that fun is also fuel. Express yourself freely, whether through art, laughter, or connecting with someone who inspires you. Capricorn, allowing joy into your day restores balance and renews motivation for bigger goals. Delight is powerful medicine.

Affirmation & Gratitude

I am grateful for joy and creativity, trusting play and laughter to recharge my energy and inspire my path.

Capricorn
02 May 2026

Work, health, and routines are in focus today. You may feel called to reorganize your schedule, refine daily habits, or tackle unfinished tasks. Capricorn, your discipline makes you skilled at building consistency, but the stars remind you to also honor balance. Don't sacrifice well-being for productivity—efficiency grows when your body and mind are supported. Small, practical changes today can create long-term resilience and steady momentum. Prioritize what sustains you, not just what demands you.

Affirmation & Gratitude

I am grateful for supportive routines that bring health, balance, and strength into my daily life.

Capricorn
03 May 2026

Partnerships take center stage. You may be asked to compromise, cooperate, or resolve a misunderstanding. The stars encourage patience and empathy, reminding you that healthy relationships thrive when both voices are respected. Capricorn, your steadiness offers reassurance, but remember vulnerability deepens trust. Today is an opportunity to strengthen bonds, whether romantic, professional, or personal. By focusing on collaboration instead of control, you create lasting harmony. Trust that openness leads to deeper understanding and connection.

Affirmation & Gratitude

I am grateful for balanced relationships built on respect, empathy, and trust, knowing connection grows stronger through openness.

Capricorn
04 May 2026

Shared resources, financial matters, or emotional commitments may surface. The stars encourage transparency and fairness—avoid assumptions or secrecy. Capricorn, your grounded nature helps stabilize sensitive conversations. By addressing matters directly, you prevent conflict and build trust. Today is also about emotional depth; honesty with yourself is just as important as honesty with others. Facing truths now strengthens your resilience and lays foundations for greater stability in the future. Courage today brings peace tomorrow.

Affirmation & Gratitude

I am grateful for clarity and honesty in shared matters, trusting fairness creates stability and stronger connections.

Capricorn
05 May 2026

The cosmos highlights growth, learning, and exploration. You may feel pulled toward study, travel, or new perspectives that broaden your horizons. Capricorn, while routine provides comfort, stepping outside it brings fresh energy and inspiration. The stars encourage you to embrace curiosity, even if it leads you into unfamiliar territory. Growth isn't always comfortable, but it shapes wisdom. Trust that what you learn today plants seeds for long-term progress and expansion.

Affirmation & Gratitude

I am grateful for opportunities that expand my perspective, welcoming growth with courage and curiosity.

Capricorn
06 May 2026

Career and reputation are emphasized today. Recognition may come your way, or responsibilities may increase. The stars remind you that success is about integrity as much as achievement. Capricorn, your persistence and patience are admired, and today offers a chance to refine your long-term goals. Ask yourself whether your current path truly aligns with your deeper purpose. Lead with humility, and you'll build not just success, but a respected legacy.

Affirmation & Gratitude

I am grateful for recognition of my efforts, trusting patience and integrity to create lasting success.

Capricorn
07 May 2026

Friendships and communities take the spotlight. The cosmos encourages you to lean on your network for support, inspiration, or collaboration. Capricorn, independence is your strength, but today reminds you that connection multiplies opportunities. A friend's perspective may open new doors or spark ideas you hadn't considered. Cherish the relationships that uplift you—they are part of the foundation that carries you through challenges and toward your dreams. Connection is strength, not weakness.

Affirmation & Gratitude

I am grateful for supportive friendships and communities, knowing shared vision and encouragement enrich my life.

Capricorn
08 May 2026

Capricorn, rest and reflection are emphasized today. You may feel mentally or emotionally drained, making solitude essential. The stars encourage you to step back from demands, recharge, and reconnect with your inner compass. Journaling, meditation, or quiet time in nature will provide clarity. Capricorn, you sometimes push through exhaustion, but today's energy reminds you that renewal comes from stillness. Trust that taking a pause doesn't slow your progress—it strengthens it. Inner alignment is your true power now.

Affirmation & Gratitude

I am grateful for the healing power of rest, trusting quiet moments to restore my clarity and strength.

Capricorn
09 May 2026

The Sun highlights your sense of identity and personal expression. You may feel called to show the world who you truly are. The stars remind you that authenticity is magnetic—it draws the right people and opportunities. Capricorn, when you live your truth, you create space for others to do the same. Today, embrace your unique strengths without apology. By stepping into your power, you set the tone for meaningful progress ahead.

Affirmation & Gratitude

I am grateful for the courage to live authentically, trusting my truth to guide me toward aligned opportunities.

Capricorn
10 May 2026

Finances and self-worth come into focus. You may be prompted to review your budget, make an investment, or rethink your money mindset. The stars encourage balance between security and enjoyment. Capricorn, you're skilled at building stability, but remember abundance is not only financial—it's also found in gratitude and fulfillment. Aligning your resources with your values ensures both prosperity and peace. Today is about making choices that reflect both practicality and purpose.

Affirmation & Gratitude

I am grateful for financial wisdom and self-worth, knowing aligned choices create security and fulfillment.

Capricorn
11 May 2026

Communication is highlighted today. The stars suggest conversations may reveal insights or open opportunities. Capricorn, your voice carries influence—use it thoughtfully. Balance logic with empathy; listening is just as important as speaking. This is an excellent day for writing, teaching, or sharing ideas publicly. Don't underestimate the impact of your steady words—they may reach further than expected. Clear, authentic dialogue today strengthens bonds and creates pathways for future growth.

Affirmation & Gratitude

I am grateful for meaningful communication, trusting my words and listening skills to build connection and clarity.

Capricorn
12 May 2026

Home and family life take center stage. You may feel called to nurture your space, reconnect with loved ones, or resolve domestic matters. The stars encourage you to create peace at home, knowing it supports your ambitions. Capricorn, stability in your sanctuary allows you to pursue goals with confidence. Whether through practical improvements or heartfelt conversations, focus on grounding your roots. Strong foundations create strength for everything else you build.

Affirmation & Gratitude

I am grateful for the peace of my home and family, knowing strong roots support my dreams.

Capricorn
13 May 2026

Joy and creativity fill the air. The stars encourage you to step into hobbies, romance, or playful expression. Capricorn, you often prioritize duty, but today is about celebrating what makes you feel alive. Fun is not frivolous—it's nourishment for your soul. Express yourself without judgment, whether through laughter, art, or love. Today's lightness inspires resilience for the heavier tasks ahead. Embrace delight—it's just as important as discipline.

Affirmation & Gratitude

I am grateful for joy and creativity, embracing play as fuel for my spirit and inspiration for my journey.

Capricorn
14 May 2026

Work, health, and routines are emphasized today. You may feel called to refine your daily schedule or focus on well-being. The stars remind you that consistency, not perfection, creates lasting results. Capricorn, your discipline makes you excellent at building supportive habits—lean into that strength. Even small changes today can ripple into long-term benefits. Prioritize what sustains your energy and peace rather than only what demands your effort. Balance is your ally now.

Affirmation & Gratitude

I am grateful for supportive routines that nurture my body and mind, creating balance, strength, and vitality.

Capricorn
15 May 2026

Partnerships take center stage today, Capricorn. The stars encourage compromise, patience, and honest dialogue. You may feel tested in a relationship, but remember, balance is key—your needs matter, yet so do theirs. Your steadiness offers reassurance, but don't shy away from showing vulnerability. True strength in relationships comes from trust and openness. A heartfelt conversation today may resolve tension or deepen intimacy. By approaching with empathy, you build lasting harmony and mutual respect.

Affirmation & Gratitude

I am grateful for the strength of my partnerships, trusting empathy and openness create bonds built on trust and respect.

Capricorn
16 May 2026

Shared resources, financial matters, or emotional commitments are highlighted. The stars encourage transparency—avoid secrecy or assumptions, as clarity creates stability. Capricorn, your grounded nature equips you to navigate these sensitive situations with fairness. Facing issues directly now builds security for yourself and others. Today may also bring emotional depth, asking you to release old fears around trust or control. By fostering honesty, you transform potential conflicts into opportunities for growth and deeper connection.

Affirmation & Gratitude

I am grateful for honesty and fairness in shared matters, trusting clarity builds strength and stability for all involved.

Capricorn
17 May 2026

The cosmos highlights growth and exploration. You may feel inspired to learn, travel, or broaden your perspective through new experiences. Capricorn, while stability anchors you, today encourages you to venture beyond comfort zones. Inspiration may come through study, philosophy, or unexpected conversations. These experiences may plant seeds that shape your future direction. The stars remind you that wisdom often comes from unfamiliar paths—stay open to the journey.

Affirmation & Gratitude

I am grateful for opportunities that expand my horizons, welcoming wisdom from new experiences and perspectives.

Capricorn
18 May 2026

Career and reputation are illuminated. Recognition for your efforts may arrive, or increased responsibilities may surface. Capricorn, your persistence and reliability are admired, but the stars remind you that true leadership blends confidence with humility. Refine your goals today to ensure they align with both ambition and authenticity. By leading with integrity, you set yourself apart. Today, success is measured not just in achievements, but in the legacy you're building.

Affirmation & Gratitude

I am grateful for recognition of my persistence and integrity, trusting my efforts create lasting success and respect.

Capricorn
19 May 2026

Friendships and communities take the spotlight. The stars encourage collaboration and shared vision. Someone in your circle may offer advice, inspiration, or opportunity. Capricorn, your independence is powerful, but today reminds you that connection multiplies potential. By leaning into your network, you gain perspective and encouragement that fuels progress. Cherish the bonds that uplift you—they're part of your foundation for growth, joy, and success.

Affirmation & Gratitude

I am grateful for supportive friendships and communities, trusting shared energy strengthens and uplifts me.

Capricorn
20 May 2026

Solitude and reflection are important today. The stars remind you that stillness allows insights to surface. Capricorn, your drive often keeps you focused on external achievements, but your inner compass is equally important. Pay attention to dreams, intuition, or quiet thoughts. They may carry guidance for your next steps. Rest is not wasted—it's essential fuel. Today, let silence restore clarity and prepare you for the challenges ahead.

Affirmation & Gratitude

I am grateful for peaceful reflection, trusting rest and intuition to guide my steps.

Capricorn
21 May 2026

The Sun lights up your sense of identity, giving you confidence to embrace your authentic self. Capricorn, today is about self-expression and standing firmly in your truth. When you live authentically, opportunities align naturally. The stars remind you that your presence inspires others, even when you don't realize it. This is a powerful day to honor who you are and step forward without hesitation. Authenticity is your greatest strength.

Affirmation & Gratitude
I am grateful for the courage to be authentic, trusting my truth to inspire and guide me.

Capricorn
22 May 2026

Finances and self-worth take the spotlight today. You may review budgets, consider an investment, or rethink your approach to money. The stars encourage you to balance practicality with fulfillment. Capricorn, your instinct is to secure stability, but abundance also means appreciating what you already have. Align spending and saving with your values, ensuring your resources support the life you want to build. Today's choices could shape long-term confidence and prosperity.

Affirmation & Gratitude

I am grateful for financial stability and wisdom, trusting my resources support both security and fulfillment in meaningful ways.

Capricorn
23 May 2026

Communication flows strongly today. The stars suggest conversations may carry extra importance, offering insights or opportunities. Capricorn, your words hold influence—be mindful of tone and intention. Listening deeply will be just as powerful as speaking. This is also a favorable time for writing, teaching, or sharing your perspective with a wider audience. Authentic dialogue today could resolve tension or open a new path. Trust the grounded strength of your voice.

Affirmation & Gratitude

I am grateful for the clarity and impact of my words, trusting communication to create connection and progress.

Capricorn
24 May 2026

Home and family matters rise in importance. You may feel drawn to nurture your living space, resolve domestic issues, or spend more time with loved ones. The stars remind you that peace at home strengthens every other part of your life. Capricorn, small actions—organizing, cooking, or offering heartfelt words—can create stability and comfort. By tending to your roots, you recharge your energy and fortify the foundation that supports your ambitions.

Affirmation & Gratitude

I am grateful for the peace of my home and family, knowing strong roots support my growth.

Capricorn
25 May 2026

Creativity, romance, and joy are emphasized today. The stars encourage you to explore hobbies, express your talents, or embrace playful moments. Capricorn, responsibility is part of your nature, but today asks you to lighten the load. Fun is nourishment, not indulgence. By leaning into joy, you restore balance and spark inspiration that may flow into your work later. Today, allow yourself to simply enjoy being alive.

Affirmation & Gratitude

I am grateful for joy, romance, and creativity, trusting play brings nourishment and inspiration.

Capricorn
26 May 2026

Work, health, and routines are in focus. You may feel called to refine daily systems or adopt supportive habits. The stars encourage consistency over drastic changes. Capricorn, your discipline makes you capable of steady progress. Today, focus on what strengthens your energy and brings balance to your days. Even a small shift, like adjusting sleep or planning tasks, can ripple into lasting well-being. Efficiency grows from care, not strain.

Affirmation & Gratitude

I am grateful for supportive routines that bring balance, health, and strength to my daily life.

Capricorn
27 May 2026

Relationships take the spotlight. You may be asked to compromise, resolve a misunderstanding, or deepen intimacy. The stars encourage openness and empathy—healthy partnerships thrive when both voices are heard. Capricorn, your steadiness offers security, but vulnerability strengthens bonds. Today, a heartfelt conversation could transform a dynamic, moving it toward greater harmony. By balancing strength with softness, you create trust and closeness that lasts.

Affirmation & Gratitude

I am grateful for love and respect in my partnerships, trusting openness and empathy to strengthen connection.

Capricorn
28 May 2026

Shared resources, financial agreements, or emotional commitments may surface. Transparency is essential—avoid assumptions or holding back. Capricorn, your grounded nature helps you manage these situations with fairness. Today is about clarity, honesty, and building stability for everyone involved. The stars remind you that courage to face difficult topics creates peace and trust. Addressing matters directly now prevents bigger conflicts later and strengthens your bonds.

Affirmation & Gratitude

I am grateful for courage and fairness in shared matters, trusting clarity creates stability and harmony.

Capricorn
29 May 2026

Capricorn, today highlights learning, exploration, and broadening your horizons. You may feel called to study, travel, or immerse yourself in new perspectives. The stars encourage you to stretch beyond familiar boundaries. Growth now may come from unexpected conversations, spiritual practices, or exposure to different cultures and ideas. Capricorn, you thrive on structure, but balance comes from allowing yourself to evolve. By embracing curiosity, you expand your vision and strengthen your long-term goals.

Affirmation & Gratitude

I am grateful for opportunities to grow and expand, trusting curiosity and openness bring wisdom and inspiration.

Capricorn
30 May 2026

Career and public image are in the spotlight today. Recognition may come your way, or new responsibilities may test your patience. The stars remind you that true leadership blends confidence with humility. Capricorn, your persistence and integrity are noticed by those around you—trust that your steady path creates the reputation you deserve. Today is ideal for refining long-term ambitions, ensuring they align with your authentic values and vision for success.

Affirmation & Gratitude

I am grateful for recognition of my persistence and integrity, trusting patience builds lasting respect and success.

Capricorn
31 May 2026

Friendships and communities take priority as the month closes. You may feel inspired by your social circle or find opportunity through collaboration. Capricorn, independence is your strength, but today reminds you of the power of collective energy. A shared vision brings encouragement and momentum that you can't create alone. Cherish the bonds that uplift you and offer your support in return. Connection is a powerful foundation for growth and joy.

Affirmation & Gratitude

I am grateful for my friendships and communities, trusting shared energy strengthens and uplifts me.

June

2026

Capricorn
01 June 2026

Capricorn, June begins with a call to rest and reflect. The stars encourage you to step back from the noise and reconnect with your inner compass. Dreams, intuition, or subtle signs may offer guidance, so pay attention to whispers from within. You often equate progress with action, but today reminds you that stillness builds strength. By pausing, you allow clarity to surface, preparing you for the busy weeks ahead. Inner alignment creates outer power.

Affirmation & Gratitude

I am grateful for peaceful reflection, trusting stillness to renew my strength and provide guidance for the path ahead.

Capricorn
02 June 2026

The Sun highlights your individuality and self-expression. Today you may feel stronger in asserting your truth or showcasing hidden talents. The stars remind you that authenticity attracts aligned opportunities. Capricorn, your quiet confidence inspires others to embrace their own truth. This is a day to stand tall and unapologetically embody who you are. By honoring yourself, you not only advance your own journey—you also light the way for others.

Affirmation & Gratitude

I am grateful for the courage to express myself authentically, trusting my truth to guide me toward aligned opportunities.

Capricorn
03 June 2026

Finances and self-worth come into focus. The stars encourage you to review spending, saving, or investing habits with honesty. Capricorn, your natural caution is an asset, but don't let fear limit growth. Align money with values so resources support both stability and fulfillment. Today is also about recognizing your worth beyond financial security. Gratitude for what you already have paves the way for abundance to flow in new and meaningful ways.

Affirmation & Gratitude

I am grateful for the wisdom to align finances with values, trusting abundance flows where purpose and gratitude meet.

Capricorn
04 June 2026

Conversations may carry unusual weight today. The stars highlight communication, asking you to share your thoughts while also listening carefully. Misunderstandings are possible if you rush, but patience and clarity will resolve them. Capricorn, your words hold influence—use them with care and intention. This is a favorable day for teaching, writing, or important discussions. When you combine reason with empathy, your message resonates more deeply and builds stronger bonds of trust.

Affirmation & Gratitude

I am grateful for meaningful conversations, trusting clear and thoughtful words to strengthen connection and understanding.

Capricorn
05 June 2026

Home and family life take priority. You may feel called to nurture your personal space, reconnect with loved ones, or resolve domestic concerns. The stars encourage you to create harmony at home, knowing your sanctuary fuels your broader ambitions. Capricorn, peace at home allows you to pursue external goals with greater confidence. Small acts—tidying, repairing, or offering heartfelt support—create stability. Today, strengthen your roots to empower the branches of your future.

Affirmation & Gratitude

I am grateful for the peace and strength of my home, trusting harmony here supports everything I build.

Capricorn
06 June 2026

Joy, romance, and creativity take the spotlight. The stars encourage you to step away from routine and embrace what makes you feel alive. Capricorn, you may feel inspired to pursue hobbies, artistic outlets, or deeper connections in love. Fun today isn't frivolous—it's nourishment. By leaning into joy, you restore balance and spark ideas that can support bigger goals later. Today, allow yourself the freedom to simply enjoy being alive.

Affirmation & Gratitude

I am grateful for joy, love, and creativity, trusting play and laughter fuel my spirit and inspire my path.

Capricorn
07 June 2026

Work, health, and daily routines are emphasized. You may feel prompted to reorganize your schedule or refine habits. Capricorn, your discipline makes you skilled at creating sustainable systems. The stars encourage supportive adjustments—small steps that build lasting resilience. Focus on balance between productivity and self-care, ensuring your energy is preserved. Today is about efficiency rooted in well-being, not pressure. Strength grows from consistent, mindful choices that support both body and spirit.

Affirmation & Gratitude

I am grateful for supportive routines that create balance and strength, trusting small steps build lasting vitality.

Capricorn
08 June 2026

Relationships are spotlighted today. The stars encourage compromise, patience, and open dialogue. Capricorn, you may be asked to balance your needs with those of a partner, colleague, or friend. Your natural steadiness provides reassurance, but remember that true intimacy requires vulnerability. By sharing your thoughts and listening in return, you create harmony. A heartfelt exchange today could strengthen bonds or resolve lingering misunderstandings. Approach with empathy, and partnerships will flourish.

Affirmation & Gratitude

I am grateful for the love and respect in my relationships, trusting openness and empathy create lasting harmony.

Capricorn
09 June 2026

Shared resources or emotional commitments may require attention. The stars highlight trust, fairness, and clarity. Capricorn, you may need to address financial arrangements or boundaries within a partnership. Avoid secrecy; transparency brings stability. Your practical wisdom equips you to guide these conversations with balance. Today is also about emotional honesty—release fears around control and allow space for deeper connection. By facing things directly, you transform potential tension into mutual growth and security.

Affirmation & Gratitude

I am grateful for honesty and fairness in shared matters, trusting courage creates stability and trust.

Capricorn
10 June 2026

Growth and exploration are highlighted. You may feel called to study, travel, or embrace new ideas that broaden your horizons. Capricorn, your practicality ensures that experiences are not fleeting—they become stepping stones for long-term wisdom. The stars remind you that curiosity fuels expansion. By stepping outside your comfort zone, you open yourself to opportunities that enrich both personal and professional paths. Growth today may plant seeds for your future ambitions.

Affirmation & Gratitude

I am grateful for opportunities to expand my perspective, welcoming growth and wisdom through curiosity and openness.

Capricorn
11 June 2026

Career and reputation take center stage. Recognition may arrive, or increased responsibilities could demand focus. Capricorn, your persistence and patience are admired, but the stars remind you that true leadership blends integrity with humility. Today is ideal for refining goals, ensuring they reflect both ambition and authenticity. Your steady example inspires others to trust and follow you. Success today is not about loud achievement—it's about consistent, respected progress.

Affirmation & Gratitude

I am grateful for recognition of my persistence and integrity, trusting patience builds meaningful success and respect.

Capricorn
12 June 2026

Friendships and communities are emphasized. The stars encourage collaboration and connection. Capricorn, your independence is a strength, but today reminds you of the power of teamwork. Someone in your circle may inspire you or open a door to opportunity. Cherish the bonds that support and uplift you. Connection isn't weakness—it's a foundation for success. By leaning into shared vision, you multiply possibilities that wouldn't appear on your own.

Affirmation & Gratitude

I am grateful for supportive friendships and communities, trusting shared energy multiplies opportunities and joy.

Capricorn
13 June 2026

The cosmos calls for solitude and rest. You may feel drained from constant demands, making reflection essential. Capricorn, slowing down is not wasted time—it allows you to reconnect with your intuition. Dreams, meditation, or journaling may reveal insights guiding your next steps. The stars remind you that inner alignment builds outer strength. By pausing now, you recharge your energy for challenges ahead. Trust the wisdom found in silence.

Affirmation & Gratitude

I am grateful for quiet moments of reflection, trusting rest restores clarity and strength.

Capricorn
14 June 2026

The Sun highlights your individuality and self-expression. Capricorn, today is about embracing your authentic self and standing confidently in your truth. The stars remind you that your presence inspires others—living authentically encourages them to do the same. Share your talents, values, or voice without fear. By honoring your uniqueness, you naturally attract the right people and opportunities. Today is a day to shine unapologetically and own your story.

Affirmation & Gratitude

I am grateful for the courage to express myself authentically, trusting my truth attracts aligned opportunities and

Capricorn
15 June 2026

Finances and self-worth rise into focus. You may feel called to reevaluate spending, saving, or how your resources reflect your values. The stars encourage you to seek balance—security is important, but fulfillment matters too. Capricorn, you excel at building stability, but today reminds you that abundance includes gratitude, joy, and meaningful use of resources. A wise choice now could strengthen both financial confidence and your sense of empowerment. Align money with purpose.

Affirmation & Gratitude

I am grateful for financial wisdom and security, trusting aligned choices bring both stability and fulfillment.

Capricorn
16 June 2026

Communication is emphasized today. Conversations may hold more depth than usual, offering clarity or revealing hidden truths. Capricorn, your words have weight—use them with intention and patience. Listening carefully will be just as important as speaking. This is also a powerful day for writing, teaching, or presenting ideas. When you combine reason with empathy, you create breakthroughs. Trust your steady, thoughtful voice—it has the power to influence and inspire others.

Affirmation & Gratitude

I am grateful for the clarity and power of my words, trusting communication strengthens bonds and opens opportunities.

Capricorn
17 June 2026

Home and family life come into focus. You may feel called to nurture your personal space or resolve domestic matters. The stars encourage harmony within your sanctuary, knowing it supports all your wider ambitions. Capricorn, your drive often pulls you outward, but peace at home provides the strength for success. Small improvements—decluttering, conversations, or shared meals—bring comfort and stability. Today is about grounding yourself where your roots give life to everything else.

Affirmation & Gratitude

I am grateful for the peace of my home and family, knowing harmony here strengthens every step I take.

Capricorn
18 June 2026

Creativity, joy, and romance light up today. The stars encourage you to embrace play, laughter, or artistic expression. Capricorn, responsibilities are important, but so is fun. Today, inspiration flows when you let go of rigid expectations and follow what excites your spirit. A spark of creativity could later transform into something practical and lasting. By nourishing joy, you replenish energy for the goals that matter most. Delight is nourishment, not distraction.

Affirmation & Gratitude
I am grateful for joy and creativity, trusting playfulness strengthens my spirit and fuels inspiration.

Capricorn
19 June 2026

Work, health, and routines are highlighted. You may feel urged to refine daily habits or reorganize responsibilities. Capricorn, your discipline helps you build consistency, but balance is just as important as effort. The stars remind you that small, sustainable changes create more impact than sweeping shifts. Today, focus on supportive systems that preserve energy and bring balance. By investing in your well-being, you strengthen the foundation needed for bigger dreams.

Affirmation & Gratitude

I am grateful for supportive routines that nurture my body and mind, building balance, strength, and resilience.

Capricorn
20 June 2026

Partnerships take center stage. You may be asked to compromise, negotiate, or lean into cooperation. The stars encourage openness and empathy. Capricorn, your steadiness is a gift in relationships, but showing vulnerability deepens connection. Today is an opportunity to resolve tension or strengthen intimacy. By balancing your needs with others', you create healthier, more resilient bonds. Remember: true partnership is about shared respect, not control.

Affirmation & Gratitude

I am grateful for the love and balance in my relationships, trusting empathy and honesty to strengthen connection.

Capricorn
21 June 2026

Shared resources and deeper emotional matters may surface. The stars encourage transparency—whether financial, practical, or personal. Capricorn, your grounded nature helps stabilize these conversations with fairness. Avoid avoiding—addressing issues directly prevents misunderstandings. This is also a day for emotional honesty; acknowledging vulnerabilities brings strength. By fostering clarity, you transform complexity into stability and trust. Today, courage creates peace.

Affirmation & Gratitude

I am grateful for honesty and fairness in shared matters, trusting clarity builds stability and trust.

Capricorn
22 June 2026

Growth and expansion are spotlighted today. You may feel drawn to new learning, spiritual exploration, or fresh experiences that broaden your horizons. Capricorn, while stability anchors you, the stars remind you that wisdom often lies beyond routine. A conversation, book, or journey could spark fresh inspiration. By staying curious, you open pathways to opportunities that align with your long-term vision. Today is about stretching beyond comfort zones and trusting discovery.

Affirmation & Gratitude

I am grateful for opportunities to expand my perspective, trusting curiosity and openness to guide me toward wisdom and growth.

Capricorn
23 June 2026

Career and reputation rise to the forefront. Recognition may arrive, or you may be asked to take on leadership. Capricorn, your persistence and reliability shine, but the stars remind you that true influence grows through integrity and humility. Today, refine your ambitions to ensure they align with your values. Success earned steadily endures, while shortcuts fade. Step forward with quiet confidence—you inspire others more than you realize.

Affirmation & Gratitude

I am grateful for recognition of my dedication and integrity, trusting patience builds lasting success and respect.

Capricorn
24 June 2026

Friendships and community are highlighted. The stars encourage you to engage with your circle, collaborate, or contribute to a shared vision. Capricorn, while independence fuels you, teamwork multiplies opportunity. A friend's advice or support may spark a breakthrough. Today is about connection—cherish the bonds that uplift you. By leaning into community, you gain both inspiration and encouragement to continue building your dreams.

Affirmation & Gratitude

I am grateful for the support of friendships and communities, trusting shared energy strengthens and inspires me.

Capricorn
25 June 2026

Solitude and reflection are vital today. You may feel drained from constant responsibilities, making rest essential. The stars remind you that stillness offers clarity no rush can provide. Capricorn, slowing down is not weakness—it's renewal. Dreams or intuition may reveal messages that help guide your choices. By creating space for quiet, you reconnect with yourself and restore energy for the days ahead. Silence today is a powerful teacher.

Affirmation & Gratitude

I am grateful for quiet reflection, trusting rest restores clarity, peace, and strength.

Capricorn
26 June 2026

The Sun highlights your sense of self and expression. Capricorn, today is about owning your truth unapologetically. The stars encourage you to shine by living authentically, showing your talents, and expressing your values with confidence. When you embrace your uniqueness, the right people and opportunities naturally align. By honoring yourself, you inspire others to honor themselves too. This is a day for confidence rooted in integrity.

Affirmation & Gratitude

I am grateful for the courage to live authentically, trusting my truth to guide me toward aligned opportunities.

Capricorn
27 June 2026

Finances and self-worth take center stage. The stars encourage you to review money habits and align them with your deeper values. Capricorn, your discipline makes you excellent at building security, but fulfillment matters too. Today is about balance—saving, earning, and enjoying life in ways that feel purposeful. Abundance flows when you appreciate what you already have. Gratitude strengthens prosperity and confidence.

Affirmation & Gratitude

I am grateful for the balance of financial stability and fulfillment, trusting abundance flows when I align with purpose.

Capricorn
28 June 2026

Communication is emphasized. The stars suggest conversations may hold significance, offering clarity or new insights. Capricorn, your words carry influence—speak with patience and empathy. Listening will be as important as sharing. Today is favorable for writing, teaching, or presenting. Don't underestimate the impact of your grounded perspective—it may reach further than you expect. Dialogue today creates bridges of trust and possibility.

Affirmation & Gratitude

I am grateful for meaningful conversations, trusting my words and listening skills to build connection and clarity.

Capricorn
29 June 2026

Home and family life rise in importance. You may feel called to nurture your personal sanctuary or address domestic matters. Capricorn, peace within your home supports your outer ambitions. The stars encourage you to invest energy into strengthening these roots—through practical improvements or heartfelt exchanges. Harmony here fortifies every other step you take. Focus on creating stability where it matters most.

Affirmation & Gratitude

I am grateful for the peace and strength of my home and family, trusting harmony here supports all I build.

Capricorn
30 June 2026

Creativity and joy take the spotlight as June closes. Capricorn, you may feel drawn to romance, hobbies, or playful expression. The stars remind you that fun is nourishment for your spirit, not indulgence. Allow yourself to step away from responsibility and embrace delight. Inspiration flows when you are lighthearted, and today's sparks may fuel future goals. Balance seriousness with joy—it keeps you resilient and inspired.

Affirmation & Gratitude

I am grateful for joy and creativity, trusting playfulness nourishes my spirit and fuels inspiration.

July
2026

Capricorn
01 July 2026

Capricorn, July begins with a focus on work, health, and routines. You may feel compelled to reorganize your schedule, refine habits, or address responsibilities with renewed energy. The stars encourage you to pursue balance—efficiency should not come at the expense of well-being. Small, consistent changes create long-lasting results. Capricorn, your discipline makes you excellent at sustaining systems, but ensure they also nurture your body and spirit. Today, progress is found in mindful adjustments, not in perfectionism.

Affirmation & Gratitude

I am grateful for supportive routines that create balance, trusting steady improvements strengthen my body, mind, and spirit.

Capricorn
02 July 2026

Partnerships come into focus today. You may need to compromise, cooperate, or navigate a sensitive conversation. The stars remind you that healthy relationships are built on respect, balance, and open communication. Capricorn, your reliability is a gift, but remember vulnerability deepens connection. By expressing yourself honestly and listening with empathy, you create trust. A moment of openness today could transform a bond and strengthen the foundation of your most meaningful relationships.

Affirmation & Gratitude

I am grateful for balanced and respectful relationships, trusting openness and empathy build harmony and strength.

Capricorn
03 July 2026

Shared resources, finances, or emotional commitments may surface. Transparency is essential—the stars warn against assumptions or avoiding important discussions. Capricorn, your grounded approach helps you stabilize matters with fairness and practicality. By addressing things clearly now, you prevent future complications. This is also a day for emotional honesty; acknowledging fears around control or vulnerability creates freedom. Courage to face the truth today builds resilience, trust, and security for the long term.

Affirmation & Gratitude

I am grateful for clarity and courage in shared matters, trusting honesty creates stability and peace.

Capricorn
04 July 2026

Growth and exploration are highlighted. The stars encourage you to step outside routine and embrace opportunities that broaden your perspective. Whether through study, travel, or conversations, inspiration may arrive in unexpected ways. Capricorn, you thrive on structure, but flexibility today brings wisdom. This is not about abandoning responsibility but about enriching your vision. Curiosity fuels growth, and what you discover now could guide long-term goals. Trust that expansion strengthens your foundations.

Affirmation & Gratitude

I am grateful for opportunities to expand my horizons, trusting curiosity and openness bring wisdom.

Capricorn
05 July 2026

Career and public reputation rise to the surface. Recognition may come, or increased responsibilities may demand your focus. Capricorn, your persistence and integrity are noticed, but the stars remind you to lead with humility. Today is ideal for refining your ambitions and ensuring they align with both purpose and values. Success built steadily lasts longer than shortcuts. Trust your patient approach—it's what sets you apart and strengthens your legacy.

Affirmation & Gratitude

I am grateful for recognition of my persistence and integrity, trusting patience and purpose create lasting success.

Capricorn
06 July 2026

Friendships and communities are emphasized today. The stars encourage collaboration, shared vision, and connection. Capricorn, independence is your strength, but today reminds you of the power of teamwork. Someone in your circle may offer inspiration or open a new door. Connection multiplies opportunities that may not come alone. Cherish your tribe—it's part of your foundation for joy, resilience, and progress. Today, collective energy fuels growth.

Affirmation & Gratitude

I am grateful for supportive friendships and communities, trusting shared energy multiplies opportunities and joy.

Capricorn
07 July 2026

Rest and reflection take priority. Capricorn, the stars remind you that stillness restores clarity and strength. You may feel called to step back, recharge, and reconnect with your inner compass. Dreams or intuition may bring valuable insights—pay attention to subtle messages. By pausing now, you prepare for the next cycle with renewed energy. Rest is not wasted time—it is preparation for meaningful progress. Silence strengthens your spirit today.

Affirmation & Gratitude

I am grateful for peaceful moments of rest, trusting reflection restores clarity and strength.

Capricorn
08 July 2026

Capricorn, the Sun highlights your individuality and self-expression today. You may feel a strong pull to assert your truth or showcase your talents. The stars encourage authenticity—don't dim yourself to fit into expectations. By living in alignment with your values, you attract opportunities that reflect your true path. Capricorn, your grounded nature gives your voice power; when you share from a place of integrity, others listen. Today is a day for unapologetic confidence and self-belief.

Affirmation & Gratitude

I am grateful for the courage to express myself authentically, trusting my truth to guide me toward aligned opportunities.

Capricorn
09 July 2026

Finances and self-worth are emphasized. You may review budgets, make decisions about investments, or reflect on how resources support your goals. The stars encourage balance—security matters, but so does fulfillment. Capricorn, you're skilled at building stability, but remember abundance also means appreciating what you already have. Align money decisions with your values for deeper peace. Today, financial clarity brings empowerment and sets the stage for sustainable growth.

Affirmation & Gratitude

I am grateful for financial wisdom and security, trusting abundance flows when I align money with my values.

Capricorn
10 July 2026

Communication is highlighted today. Conversations may carry more depth than usual, offering breakthroughs or clarity. Capricorn, your words carry influence, so speak with care and listen deeply. This is also a favorable day for writing, teaching, or sharing your perspective publicly. The stars remind you that blending empathy with reason ensures your message resonates widely. Authentic dialogue today can resolve tension and open new doors. Trust your steady voice—it inspires trust.

Affirmation & Gratitude

I am grateful for the clarity and power of my words, trusting communication builds connection and growth.

Capricorn
11 July 2026

Home and family life take priority. The stars encourage you to nurture your space or strengthen family connections. Capricorn, your ambitions thrive when your roots are steady. Small improvements—decluttering, repairing, or sharing meaningful time—create harmony and support. Today is about grounding yourself where your foundations lie. Peace at home fuels confidence in the wider world. By tending to your personal sanctuary, you strengthen the base that carries all your dreams.

Affirmation & Gratitude

I am grateful for the peace of my home and family, trusting strong roots support my life.

Capricorn
12 July 2026

Joy, romance, and creativity light up your day. The stars encourage you to explore hobbies, laughter, or connection with loved ones. Capricorn, responsibilities may press, but today is about embracing delight without guilt. Fun is nourishment—it recharges your spirit and restores motivation. By allowing yourself to play, you open channels of inspiration that fuel future goals. Balance is found when duty and joy coexist. Celebrate the beauty of the present moment.

Affirmation & Gratitude

I am grateful for joy and creativity, trusting play nourishes my spirit and sparks inspiration.

Capricorn
13 July 2026

Work, health, and routines are emphasized today. The stars encourage supportive adjustments rather than sweeping overhauls. Capricorn, your discipline makes you excellent at building sustainable systems. Focus on efficiency without compromising well-being. Even one small improvement—better planning, healthier food, or clearer boundaries—can create lasting resilience. Today, remember that consistency builds strength over time. Progress is not about perfection but about daily actions that align with your long-term goals.

Affirmation & Gratitude

I am grateful for supportive routines that bring health, balance, and strength to my daily life.

Capricorn
14 July 2026

Relationships are spotlighted. You may need to compromise, cooperate, or navigate an important conversation. The stars remind you that healthy partnerships thrive on empathy, trust, and mutual respect. Capricorn, your steadiness provides security, but vulnerability creates intimacy. By balancing strength with softness, you strengthen bonds. A heartfelt exchange today could transform a dynamic and bring you closer to someone important. Today is about harmony through openness.

Affirmation & Gratitude

I am grateful for the love and respect in my relationships, trusting openness builds deeper harmony and connection.

Capricorn
15 July 2026

Shared resources, finances, or emotional bonds may surface today. The stars encourage honesty and clarity—avoid assumptions or leaving matters unresolved. Capricorn, your grounded approach equips you to stabilize situations with fairness. This is also a day to release fears of control, allowing balance in partnerships. By addressing matters openly, you strengthen trust and create security for the long term. Transparency is not just practical—it is healing. Courage to face truths now transforms connections.

Affirmation & Gratitude

I am grateful for clarity and fairness in shared matters, trusting honesty builds trust and stability.

Capricorn
16 July 2026

Growth and exploration are highlighted. You may feel restless for new knowledge or experiences that stretch beyond your usual boundaries. Capricorn, your disciplined nature thrives on routine, but today the stars remind you that curiosity fuels wisdom. A conversation, study, or unexpected adventure may inspire long-term changes. Be open to opportunities, even if they don't fit your plans perfectly. Expansion today creates the foundation for tomorrow's vision.

Affirmation & Gratitude

I am grateful for opportunities that broaden my perspective, trusting curiosity and openness bring wisdom and growth.

Capricorn
17 July 2026

Career and public image rise to prominence. Recognition may come, or responsibilities may weigh heavier than usual. Capricorn, your persistence and patience are noticed by others, but the stars remind you that leadership requires humility as much as authority. Today is a chance to refine your ambitions to reflect purpose and authenticity. Your steady influence inspires others—trust that your legacy is built one consistent step at a time.

Affirmation & Gratitude

I am grateful for recognition of my persistence and integrity, trusting patience and purpose create lasting success.

Capricorn
18 July 2026

Friendships and community connections are emphasized. The stars encourage you to engage with your network and collaborate on shared visions. Capricorn, independence defines you, but today's energy reminds you of the power of teamwork. A friend may offer insight or encouragement that sparks fresh direction. Cherish the people who uplift you; they are part of your foundation for resilience and joy. Shared energy multiplies possibilities.

Affirmation & Gratitude

I am grateful for my supportive friendships and communities, trusting shared vision and energy fuel growth.

Capricorn
19 July 2026

Solitude and reflection are important today. You may feel drained or contemplative, making rest essential. The stars remind you that inner renewal is just as important as outward achievement. Capricorn, quiet time brings clarity and allows intuition to speak. Pay attention to subtle insights—they may guide your next steps. By creating space for stillness, you prepare for stronger forward movement. Rest is not wasted—it is preparation.

Affirmation & Gratitude

I am grateful for quiet moments of rest, trusting reflection restores clarity and strength.

Capricorn
20 July 2026

The Sun highlights your individuality and self-expression. Capricorn, today is about confidence in your authentic self. The stars encourage you to share your talents, speak your truth, and live in alignment with your values. By embracing who you are unapologetically, you attract opportunities that reflect your path. Your authenticity also inspires others to embrace themselves. Today, shine without fear—you are at your most powerful when you are real.

Affirmation & Gratitude

I am grateful for the courage to live authentically, trusting my truth attracts aligned opportunities.

Capricorn
21 July 2026

Finances and self-worth come into focus. You may reassess spending, savings, or how money aligns with your values. Capricorn, the stars remind you that abundance is not just financial—it is also gratitude, confidence, and fulfillment. By making mindful choices now, you strengthen your foundation. Align resources with what truly matters, and you'll find peace in both security and meaning. Today is about empowerment through clarity and gratitude.

Affirmation & Gratitude

I am grateful for the wisdom to align finances with values, trusting abundance flows when purpose leads.

Capricorn
22 July 2026

Communication is emphasized today. You may find yourself in meaningful conversations that reveal new insights or resolve misunderstandings. Capricorn, your words carry weight, and the stars encourage you to blend reason with empathy. Listen carefully—sometimes the wisdom you seek arrives through others. This is also a strong day for writing or teaching, as your grounded perspective inspires trust. Authentic dialogue opens doors you didn't expect. Use your voice wisely—it's a powerful tool.

Affirmation & Gratitude

I am grateful for meaningful communication, trusting my words and listening skills build clarity and stronger connections.

Capricorn
23 July 2026

Home and family matters take priority. The stars encourage you to nurture your sanctuary, whether through practical improvements or heartfelt conversations. Capricorn, peace at home supports all your outer ambitions. Even small gestures—cooking, repairing, or spending quality time—can create harmony. Your ambitions thrive when your roots are steady. Today, strengthen the foundation that carries you through challenges and toward success. Harmony at home is strength in every other area of life.

Affirmation & Gratitude

I am grateful for the peace of my home and family, trusting harmony here strengthens all I build.

Capricorn
24 July 2026

Joy, romance, and creativity take the spotlight. The stars encourage you to step into play, expression, or love without guilt. Capricorn, you often prioritize responsibility, but today reminds you that joy is not frivolous—it's fuel. By leaning into what excites your heart, you spark inspiration that may ripple into your professional life too. Today is about celebrating the beauty of being alive. Fun replenishes your energy for bigger dreams.

Affirmation & Gratitude

I am grateful for joy, romance, and creativity, trusting play nourishes my spirit and inspires my path.

Capricorn
25 July 2026

Work, health, and routines are highlighted. The stars encourage you to refine habits and systems that support long-term strength. Capricorn, your discipline ensures progress, but balance matters just as much as effort. Avoid overloading yourself—efficiency grows when you prioritize well-being alongside productivity. Today is an opportunity to design sustainable structures that carry you forward. By investing in your body and daily practices, you secure the foundation for ambitious goals.

Affirmation & Gratitude

I am grateful for supportive routines that bring balance, health, and strength to my days.

Capricorn
26 July 2026

Relationships take center stage. The stars encourage compromise, patience, and empathy. Capricorn, your steadiness brings reassurance, but vulnerability deepens trust. By balancing strength with openness, you nurture healthier bonds. A heartfelt conversation today may resolve tension or bring greater intimacy. Remember, partnership thrives on respect and honesty. Today is about leaning into connection and recognizing that love grows stronger when both voices are valued.

Affirmation & Gratitude

I am grateful for the love and respect in my relationships, trusting empathy and openness create harmony.

Capricorn
27 July 2026

Shared resources or emotional bonds may need attention. Financial agreements or trust issues could surface, and the stars encourage transparency. Capricorn, your grounded wisdom equips you to bring stability to these situations. By addressing matters openly, you create fairness and security. This is also a powerful day for emotional honesty—facing vulnerabilities builds strength and deepens trust. Courage in sensitive conversations today transforms challenges into opportunities for stronger bonds.

Affirmation & Gratitude

I am grateful for clarity and fairness in shared matters, trusting honesty creates stability and peace.

Capricorn
28 July 2026

Growth and exploration are highlighted. You may feel inspired to study, travel, or embrace a new perspective. Capricorn, your love of structure anchors you, but today the stars remind you to embrace flexibility. Curiosity fuels wisdom, and stepping into the unknown creates opportunities. What you learn now may influence long-term direction. Stay open to experiences that enrich both heart and mind. Expansion strengthens your vision for the future.

Affirmation & Gratitude

I am grateful for opportunities to expand my perspective, trusting curiosity leads me toward wisdom.

Capricorn
29 July 2026

Career and reputation are spotlighted. Recognition may arrive, or responsibilities may increase. Capricorn, your persistence and patience are noticed, but today the stars remind you to lead with humility. Refine your ambitions to reflect not only success but also purpose. A legacy built on integrity endures far longer than one built on appearance. Step into leadership with quiet confidence—you inspire others by example more than by words.

Affirmation & Gratitude

I am grateful for recognition of my persistence and integrity, trusting purpose and patience create lasting success.

Capricorn
30 July 2026

Friendships and community are emphasized. The stars encourage you to lean on your network for support and inspiration. Capricorn, while independence defines you, collaboration multiplies opportunity. Someone in your circle may offer encouragement that sparks fresh momentum. Today, connection is strength—it gives you the energy to pursue bigger goals. Cherish the people who uplift you; they are part of your foundation for joy and resilience.

Affirmation & Gratitude

I am grateful for my supportive friendships and communities, trusting shared energy multiplies opportunities.

Capricorn
31 July 2026

The month closes with rest and reflection. Capricorn, the stars encourage you to pause, recharge, and gather wisdom from within. You often measure success by external progress, but today's gift is inner clarity. Dreams, meditation, or quiet time may reveal guidance for the next cycle. Stillness restores energy for the ambitions ahead. By honoring rest, you prepare yourself for stronger strides in August. Renewal is your hidden superpower today.

Affirmation & Gratitude

I am grateful for peaceful moments of rest, trusting reflection renews my spirit and guides my next steps.

August 2026

Capricorn
01 August 2026

Capricorn, August begins with the Sun shining on your individuality and self-expression. You may feel called to assert yourself more boldly or share talents you've kept quiet. The stars encourage authenticity—your truth attracts the right opportunities. Capricorn, your grounded nature gives weight to your words and actions, inspiring others when you live authentically. Today is a powerful time to own your story unapologetically. By showing up as yourself, you create alignment in all areas.

Affirmation & Gratitude

I am grateful for the courage to live authentically, trusting my truth attracts aligned people and opportunities.

Capricorn
02 August 2026

Finances and self-worth are highlighted. The stars encourage you to review budgets, earning potential, or how you value yourself. Capricorn, you excel at building stability, but remember prosperity isn't only about money—it's also about fulfillment. Align resources with your deeper values so financial decisions bring peace as well as security. Gratitude for what you already have strengthens abundance. Today's clarity could set the tone for wise long-term choices.

Affirmation & Gratitude

I am grateful for financial wisdom and self-worth, trusting abundance flows when I align money with purpose.

Capricorn
03 August 2026

Conversations hold weight today. The stars highlight communication—whether resolving a conflict, teaching, or sharing ideas. Capricorn, your words carry influence; be intentional with them. Listen carefully, as guidance may come from unexpected sources. Writing or public speaking may also feel particularly impactful now. Your steady perspective inspires trust when paired with empathy. Today is about creating clarity through dialogue—bridges are built when communication is honest and respectful.

Affirmation & Gratitude

I am grateful for the clarity and impact of my words, trusting communication builds connection and understanding.

Capricorn
04 August 2026

Home and family life take priority. The stars encourage nurturing your sanctuary and strengthening bonds with loved ones. Capricorn, your ambitions soar higher when your roots are strong. Small acts—cleaning, cooking, or offering supportive words—bring harmony. Today is a reminder that stability at home provides the strength you need for success outside. By investing in your foundation, you create balance and resilience that fuels your dreams.

Affirmation & Gratitude

I am grateful for the peace and strength of my home and family, trusting harmony here supports my greater path.

Capricorn
05 August 2026

Creativity, romance, and joy are emphasized today. The stars encourage you to embrace play, hobbies, or lighthearted connection. Capricorn, responsibility is part of your nature, but joy nourishes your spirit. Fun sparks inspiration, fueling not only happiness but also your professional pursuits. Allow yourself to laugh, create, and connect—it restores balance and brings renewal. Today, let delight be your guide.

Affirmation & Gratitude

I am grateful for joy, romance, and creativity, trusting play nourishes my spirit and sparks inspiration.

Capricorn
06 August 2026

Work, health, and routines are in focus. You may feel called to refine daily systems or adopt healthier habits. Capricorn, your discipline makes you excellent at building consistency. The stars remind you that balance matters—productivity thrives when well-being is prioritized. Even small improvements ripple into long-term resilience. Today is about sustainable changes that support both ambition and energy. Progress is found in mindful adjustments, not overexertion.

Affirmation & Gratitude

I am grateful for supportive routines that nurture balance, health, and vitality, trusting steady steps build resilience.

Capricorn
07 August 2026

Relationships are spotlighted. The stars encourage compromise, patience, and empathy in partnerships. Capricorn, your reliability offers stability, but openness strengthens bonds. A heartfelt conversation today may resolve tension or bring greater intimacy. Partnerships thrive when both voices are heard and respected. By balancing strength with vulnerability, you create trust and harmony. Today, invest in connection—it's as vital as ambition.

Affirmation & Gratitude

I am grateful for the love and respect in my relationships, trusting openness and empathy create lasting harmony.

Capricorn
08 August 2026

Shared resources and emotional bonds are emphasized today. Issues around money, trust, or boundaries may arise. Capricorn, your grounded approach allows you to stabilize these matters with fairness. The stars encourage transparency—avoid secrecy or avoidance, as honesty builds long-term trust. Emotional depth may also surface, asking you to face fears of vulnerability or control. By addressing things openly, you transform challenges into opportunities for healing and stronger connections. Courage today creates peace tomorrow.

Affirmation & Gratitude

I am grateful for clarity and fairness in shared matters, trusting honesty strengthens trust and security.

Capricorn
09 August 2026

Growth and exploration are spotlighted. You may feel inspired to learn, travel, or step into experiences that stretch your perspective. Capricorn, routine grounds you, but today the stars remind you that wisdom is born from curiosity. A conversation, book, or unexpected encounter could plant seeds for future goals. By embracing opportunities outside your comfort zone, you strengthen your vision and enrich your path. Trust that new experiences will align with your purpose.

Affirmation & Gratitude

I am grateful for opportunities to expand my horizons, trusting curiosity leads me to wisdom and growth.

Capricorn
10 August 2026

Career and reputation rise to the surface. Recognition for past efforts may arrive, or increased responsibilities may call for your attention. Capricorn, your persistence and integrity shine brightest when paired with humility. The stars remind you that success built slowly and honestly creates a respected legacy. Use today to refine your ambitions, ensuring they align with your deeper values. Leadership is not about control—it's about inspiring by example.

Affirmation & Gratitude

I am grateful for recognition of my persistence and integrity, trusting patience and purpose create lasting success.

Capricorn
11 August 2026

Friendships and community connections are emphasized. The stars encourage collaboration and shared vision. Capricorn, your independence is powerful, but today reminds you that collective energy creates momentum. Someone in your circle may offer inspiration or support, helping you see possibilities you might overlook alone. Cherish your network; these bonds provide joy and resilience. By investing in community, you multiply opportunities and deepen your sense of belonging.

Affirmation & Gratitude

I am grateful for supportive friendships and communities, trusting shared vision multiplies opportunities and joy.

Capricorn
12 August 2026

Solitude and reflection are highlighted. You may feel called to withdraw from noise and reconnect with your inner self. Capricorn, your drive often pushes you forward, but today the stars remind you that stillness restores strength. Intuition may offer guidance if you listen. By resting and reflecting, you prepare for greater clarity in the days ahead. Rest is not wasted—it's an essential step in sustainable success.

Affirmation & Gratitude

I am grateful for quiet moments of reflection, trusting rest restores clarity and strength.

Capricorn
13 August 2026

The Sun illuminates your individuality and self-expression. Capricorn, today encourages you to embrace authenticity and share your talents boldly. When you live in alignment with your truth, opportunities align with ease. Your grounded confidence inspires others to do the same. The stars remind you that being unapologetically yourself is your greatest strength. Today, step forward without hesitation—you are at your most powerful when you shine authentically.

Affirmation & Gratitude

I am grateful for the courage to live authentically, trusting my truth attracts aligned people and opportunities.

Capricorn
14 August 2026

Finances and self-worth come into focus. You may feel urged to reassess spending, saving, or investments. Capricorn, you're excellent at creating stability, but fulfillment matters too. The stars encourage aligning money decisions with your deeper values. Gratitude for what you already have strengthens abundance. Today is about empowerment—seeing yourself as worthy of both security and joy. By making clear financial choices, you build confidence and peace.

Affirmation & Gratitude

I am grateful for financial wisdom and self-worth, trusting abundance flows when values and purpose guide me.

Capricorn
15 August 2026

Capricorn, communication is emphasized today. The stars encourage you to express your thoughts clearly and listen with equal care. Conversations may carry unusual depth, revealing hidden truths or sparking important realizations. Writing, teaching, or sharing your perspective publicly could be especially impactful. Capricorn, your steady reasoning gives weight to your words, but remember that empathy makes them resonate. Today is about building bridges through authentic dialogue. Use your voice wisely—it has the power to inspire.

Affirmation & Gratitude

I am grateful for the clarity and influence of my words, trusting communication builds trust, understanding, and growth.

Capricorn
16 August 2026

Home and family matters take priority. You may feel drawn to nurture your space or address unresolved dynamics. Capricorn, peace at home strengthens your ability to pursue ambitions in the wider world. The stars encourage small actions—tidying, organizing, or heartfelt connection—that create comfort and stability. Your roots matter; they give you the strength to stand tall. Today, tending to your sanctuary grounds you for what lies ahead.

Affirmation & Gratitude

I am grateful for the peace of my home and family, trusting strong roots support all I build.

Capricorn
17 August 2026

Creativity, romance, and joy take center stage. The stars encourage you to embrace hobbies, playful expression, or heartfelt connection. Capricorn, responsibilities often weigh heavily, but today is about nourishing your spirit. Fun is not wasted—it restores balance and energy. Inspiration that arises through joy may fuel your professional goals later. By celebrating the lighter side of life, you strengthen your resilience and deepen your sense of fulfillment.

Affirmation & Gratitude

I am grateful for joy, romance, and creativity, trusting playfulness fuels inspiration and balance.

Capricorn
18 August 2026

Work, health, and routines are emphasized. You may feel called to refine your schedule, adopt healthier habits, or tackle responsibilities more efficiently. Capricorn, your discipline makes you skilled at creating consistency, but balance is as important as productivity. The stars encourage supportive adjustments that strengthen your energy and well-being. Today, focus on sustainability—habits that align with your long-term goals and create resilience.

Affirmation & Gratitude

I am grateful for supportive routines that nurture balance, strength, and health, trusting small steps create lasting impact.

Capricorn
19 August 2026

Relationships take the spotlight today. The stars highlight cooperation, compromise, and mutual respect. Capricorn, your steadiness provides security, but intimacy deepens when you allow vulnerability. A heartfelt exchange may resolve misunderstandings or strengthen bonds. Today is about finding harmony through openness—ensuring both your needs and the needs of others are valued. Healthy connections thrive when both voices are heard.

Affirmation & Gratitude

I am grateful for love and respect in my relationships, trusting openness and empathy create harmony and strength.

Capricorn
20 August 2026

Shared resources and emotional commitments are emphasized. You may need to clarify financial matters, boundaries, or trust within partnerships. Capricorn, your grounded wisdom equips you to stabilize situations fairly. The stars encourage honesty—avoiding issues only creates tension later. Emotional depth may also surface, offering healing if faced with courage. Today, confronting the truth creates stability for the future.

Affirmation & Gratitude

I am grateful for clarity and fairness in shared matters, trusting honesty builds trust and stability.

Capricorn
21 August 2026

Growth and exploration are spotlighted. You may feel inspired to learn, travel, or connect with new philosophies. Capricorn, while structure comforts you, today reminds you that wisdom often comes from experiences beyond routine. A new perspective may plant seeds that shape your future direction. The stars encourage you to welcome opportunities, even if they stretch you beyond comfort zones. Expansion strengthens your vision and enriches your life.

Affirmation & Gratitude

I am grateful for opportunities that expand my perspective, trusting curiosity and openness bring wisdom.

Capricorn
22 August 2026

Career and reputation are highlighted today. Recognition may come your way, or you may be asked to take on new responsibilities. Capricorn, your persistence and reliability are admired, but the stars remind you to lead with humility as well as authority. Success is not only measured in achievements but in how authentically you align with your values. By refining your ambitions today, you strengthen your legacy. Lead by example—your steadiness inspires others.

Affirmation & Gratitude

I am grateful for recognition of my persistence and integrity, trusting patience and authenticity build lasting success.

Capricorn
23 August 2026

Friendships and community connections take the spotlight. The stars encourage you to lean on your network for inspiration, advice, or collaboration. Capricorn, independence is your strength, but today reminds you that connection multiplies opportunities. A friend may offer encouragement or spark an idea that leads to progress. Cherish these bonds—they are part of your foundation for joy and resilience. Collective energy lifts you higher than you could climb alone.

Affirmation & Gratitude

I am grateful for supportive friendships and communities, trusting shared energy multiplies opportunities and joy.

Capricorn
24 August 2026

Solitude and reflection are essential today. The stars encourage you to pause, recharge, and listen to your inner compass. Capricorn, you often equate progress with external results, but today's energy reminds you that clarity is born in stillness. Pay attention to intuition, dreams, or subtle insights—they may carry guidance for your next steps. Rest is not a retreat; it is preparation for the future. Honor the silence and let wisdom surface.

Affirmation & Gratitude

I am grateful for quiet moments of reflection, trusting rest restores clarity and strength.

Capricorn
25 August 2026

The Sun illuminates your individuality and personal expression. Capricorn, today is about confidence in your authentic self. When you live unapologetically aligned with your truth, opportunities flow more easily. The stars encourage you to share talents, ideas, or values boldly. Your steady presence inspires trust, and your authenticity encourages others to embrace themselves. Today is a day to shine, not by pretending, but by simply being who you are.

Affirmation & Gratitude

I am grateful for the courage to live authentically, trusting my truth attracts the right people and opportunities.

Capricorn
26 August 2026

Finances and self-worth take center stage. You may feel prompted to review spending, income, or investments. Capricorn, your discipline makes you strong in building stability, but abundance is also about gratitude and meaningful use of resources. The stars encourage choices that support both security and fulfillment. Aligning money decisions with values creates peace and empowerment. Today, clarity about your financial path builds confidence for the long term.

Affirmation & Gratitude

I am grateful for financial wisdom and stability, trusting aligned choices create abundance and confidence.

Capricorn
27 August 2026

Communication is emphasized. Conversations may carry more importance than usual, offering clarity or new direction. Capricorn, your words carry influence, so use them thoughtfully. Listening is just as important as speaking—insight may come from unexpected sources. This is also a strong day for writing or teaching, as your steady voice inspires trust. Authentic dialogue can resolve misunderstandings or build bridges. Today, communication becomes a tool for progress and connection.

Affirmation & Gratitude

I am grateful for the clarity and impact of my words, trusting meaningful communication builds bridges.

Capricorn
28 August 2026

Home and family matters rise in importance. You may feel called to strengthen your sanctuary, resolve family dynamics, or simply create peace in your space. Capricorn, your ambitions thrive when your roots are steady. The stars encourage you to nurture your personal foundation today, whether through practical actions or emotional conversations. Harmony at home empowers everything you build in the world. Focus on creating balance where it matters most.

Affirmation & Gratitude

I am grateful for the peace of my home and family, trusting harmony here strengthens all I pursue.

Capricorn
29 August 2026

Joy, romance, and creativity take the spotlight. The stars encourage play, hobbies, or heartfelt connection. Capricorn, you often prioritize responsibility, but today is about celebrating delight as nourishment. By leaning into what makes your heart sing, you restore energy and inspiration. Fun is not wasted—it fuels you for future challenges. Today is about balance: allowing space for love, art, and laughter alongside discipline and ambition.

Affirmation & Gratitude

I am grateful for joy, romance, and creativity, trusting play nourishes my spirit and fuels inspiration.

Capricorn
30 August 2026

Work, health, and routines are emphasized. The stars encourage you to refine systems, build healthier habits, and focus on sustainability. Capricorn, your discipline makes you excellent at maintaining structure, but balance is key—well-being must be part of the plan. Even small improvements today can ripple into lasting resilience. Focus on mindful adjustments that support your body, mind, and spirit. Progress is found in steady steps, not extremes.

Affirmation & Gratitude

I am grateful for supportive routines that nurture health, balance, and resilience, trusting steady steps bring strength.

Capricorn
31 August 2026

Relationships are emphasized as the month closes. The stars highlight cooperation, compromise, and understanding. Capricorn, your reliability offers stability, but openness creates intimacy. A heartfelt exchange may resolve tension or deepen connection. Today, focus on building harmony through empathy and respect. Healthy bonds thrive when both voices are valued. By balancing strength with vulnerability, you create trust that lasts. August ends with a reminder that love is as important as ambition.

Affirmation & Gratitude

I am grateful for the love and respect in my relationships, trusting empathy builds harmony and strength.

September 2026

Capricorn
01 September 2026

Capricorn, shared resources and emotional commitments may come into focus today. Issues involving finances, joint ventures, or trust could require attention. The stars encourage transparency—avoiding conversations only builds tension. Capricorn, your grounded nature equips you to stabilize matters with fairness and practicality. This is also a day for emotional honesty. By confronting fears around control or vulnerability, you strengthen your resilience and deepen connection. Today, courage creates stability and trust for the long term.

Affirmation & Gratitude

I am grateful for honesty and fairness in shared matters, trusting courage builds trust and stability.

Capricorn
02 September 2026

Growth and exploration are emphasized. You may feel inspired to study, travel, or explore new philosophies. Capricorn, you thrive on structure, but today the stars remind you that wisdom often comes from unfamiliar paths. Curiosity is your teacher—stay open to perspectives that stretch your worldview. Inspiration now could plant seeds that guide your long-term vision. By welcoming new experiences, you enrich your spirit and strengthen your ambition.

Affirmation & Gratitude

I am grateful for opportunities to expand my perspective, trusting curiosity leads me to wisdom and growth.

Capricorn
03 September 2026

Career and reputation take the spotlight. Recognition may arrive, or responsibilities may increase. Capricorn, your persistence and integrity are noticed by others, but the stars remind you to lead with humility. Today is a chance to refine your ambitions and ensure they align with your values. True success is built step by step, rooted in authenticity. By remaining patient and consistent, you strengthen your legacy and inspire trust in others.

Affirmation & Gratitude

I am grateful for recognition of my persistence and integrity, trusting patience and authenticity create lasting success.

Capricorn
04 September 2026

Friendships and communities are highlighted today. The stars encourage collaboration and connection. Capricorn, your independence is admirable, but shared vision multiplies possibilities. A friend may offer encouragement, advice, or inspiration that sparks momentum. Leaning into community strengthens resilience and creates joy. Today is about appreciating the people who support your journey and recognizing that success is sweeter when shared.

Affirmation & Gratitude

I am grateful for supportive friendships and communities, trusting shared energy multiplies opportunity and joy.

Capricorn
05 September 2026

Solitude and reflection are emphasized. Capricorn, you may feel the need to step away from demands to rest and realign. The stars remind you that stillness restores clarity and energy. Pay attention to intuition, dreams, or quiet thoughts—they may offer guidance for your next steps. By pausing today, you prepare yourself for stronger forward movement. Rest is not retreat—it is renewal.

Affirmation & Gratitude

I am grateful for peaceful moments of rest, trusting reflection restores clarity and strength.

Capricorn
06 September 2026

The Sun highlights your individuality and self-expression. Capricorn, today is about standing tall in your truth and living authentically. By embracing who you are unapologetically, you attract opportunities that align with your values. The stars remind you that your steady confidence inspires others—your authenticity encourages them to do the same. Today is a powerful day to own your story without fear.

Affirmation & Gratitude

I am grateful for the courage to live authentically, trusting my truth attracts the right people and opportunities.

Capricorn
07 September 2026

Finances and self-worth take the spotlight. The stars encourage you to review money habits and align them with your values. Capricorn, your discipline makes you excellent at creating security, but abundance is also about gratitude and fulfillment. Today, focus on making choices that support both stability and meaning. By recognizing your worth, you empower yourself to pursue goals with confidence.

Affirmation & Gratitude

I am grateful for financial wisdom and self-worth, trusting aligned choices bring both stability and fulfillment.

Capricorn
08 September 2026

Communication is emphasized today. Conversations may reveal insights or bring opportunities, but the stars urge you to choose your words carefully. Capricorn, your grounded tone inspires trust, but empathy gives your message depth. This is a powerful day for teaching, writing, or resolving misunderstandings. Listen attentively—important guidance may come from unexpected sources. Dialogue today has the potential to heal rifts or open new pathways. Trust that your steady voice carries impact and influence.

Affirmation & Gratitude

I am grateful for the clarity and influence of my words, trusting communication builds bridges of trust and growth.

Capricorn
09 September 2026

Home and family life are in focus. You may feel the urge to improve your living space, connect with loved ones, or resolve domestic matters. The stars remind you that your ambitions soar higher when your roots feel steady. Capricorn, small gestures—tidying, cooking, or honest conversations—can create harmony. Today is about grounding yourself where your heart feels secure. Peace within your sanctuary strengthens all you build in the world beyond.

Affirmation & Gratitude

I am grateful for the peace of my home and family, trusting strong roots support my growth.

Capricorn
10 September 2026

Creativity, romance, and joy are highlighted. The stars encourage you to step into hobbies, laughter, or heartfelt connection. Capricorn, you often prioritize duty, but today is about celebrating life's lighter side. Fun isn't indulgence—it's nourishment. By embracing play, you restore balance and spark inspiration that may flow into bigger goals later. Today's delight holds wisdom—don't underestimate how powerful joy can be in fueling ambition and resilience.

Affirmation & Gratitude

I am grateful for joy, romance, and creativity, trusting play nourishes my spirit and sparks inspiration.

Capricorn
11 September 2026

Work, health, and routines take priority today. Capricorn, you may feel called to refine systems, improve efficiency, or adopt healthier habits. The stars encourage sustainability—progress comes from small, consistent steps rather than drastic changes. Your discipline is your greatest asset, but balance matters too. By investing in well-being, you create the resilience needed for long-term goals. Today is about aligning effort with self-care for true productivity.

Affirmation & Gratitude

I am grateful for supportive routines that bring balance, health, and strength to my days.

Capricorn
12 September 2026

Relationships are spotlighted. You may be asked to compromise, resolve tension, or show vulnerability. Capricorn, your reliability creates stability, but openness deepens trust. The stars encourage you to listen as much as you speak, ensuring both sides feel valued. A heartfelt conversation today could strengthen intimacy or rebuild harmony. Remember, true partnerships are nurtured with respect, honesty, and empathy. Today is about building connection, not control.

Affirmation & Gratitude

I am grateful for the love and respect in my relationships, trusting openness and empathy strengthen connection.

Capricorn
13 September 2026

Shared resources, finances, or emotional commitments may surface. Transparency is essential—the stars warn against assumptions or secrecy. Capricorn, your grounded wisdom equips you to navigate these situations with fairness. By facing matters directly, you create trust and stability for the future. This is also a powerful day for emotional honesty—acknowledging fears or vulnerabilities frees you from their hold. Courage to address the truth today transforms challenges into security.

Affirmation & Gratitude

I am grateful for clarity and fairness in shared matters, trusting honesty builds stability and peace.

Capricorn
14 September 2026

Growth and exploration are spotlighted. The stars encourage you to step outside comfort zones, whether through travel, study, or new philosophies. Capricorn, you thrive on structure, but today reminds you that wisdom is often found in the unfamiliar. Inspiration from new experiences may shape your long-term vision. By welcoming curiosity, you enrich both your inner world and your external ambitions. Expansion strengthens your path forward.

Affirmation & Gratitude

I am grateful for opportunities that expand my perspective, trusting curiosity and openness bring wisdom.

Capricorn
15 September 2026

Career and public reputation take center stage today. Recognition may come your way, or new responsibilities may require your attention. Capricorn, your persistence and patience are admired, but the stars remind you to lead with humility and integrity. True influence comes not from control, but from consistency and authenticity. Today is an opportunity to refine your goals and ensure they align with your deeper values. Legacy is built step by step.

Affirmation & Gratitude

I am grateful for recognition of my persistence and integrity, trusting patience and authenticity create lasting success.

Capricorn
16 September 2026

Friendships and community connections are emphasized. Capricorn, you may be inspired by someone in your circle, or find an opportunity through collaboration. The stars remind you that teamwork multiplies what's possible. Independence is your strength, but connection is your foundation. By leaning into shared vision, you gain both support and encouragement. Today, appreciate the people who walk beside you—they are part of your strength. Collective energy fuels progress.

Affirmation & Gratitude

I am grateful for supportive friendships and communities, trusting shared vision multiplies opportunities and joy.

Capricorn
17 September 2026

Solitude and reflection are essential today. Capricorn, the stars encourage you to step back from noise and reconnect with your inner self. Dreams, meditation, or journaling may reveal insights guiding your next steps. You often equate progress with action, but renewal comes from stillness. By pausing, you gather the clarity and energy needed for the road ahead. Rest is preparation, not retreat. Honor today's call for inner alignment.

Affirmation & Gratitude
I am grateful for peaceful moments of rest, trusting stillness restores clarity and strength.

Capricorn
18 September 2026

The Sun highlights your individuality and self-expression. Today you may feel called to embrace your authentic self more boldly. Capricorn, when you live unapologetically aligned with your truth, opportunities flow naturally. Your grounded confidence inspires others and encourages them to do the same. The stars remind you that authenticity is your greatest strength. Today is about shining as you are—without apology, without hesitation.

Affirmation & Gratitude

I am grateful for the courage to live authentically, trusting my truth attracts the right people and opportunities.

Capricorn
19 September 2026

Finances and self-worth are emphasized. The stars encourage you to reassess spending, saving, or investments. Capricorn, you're disciplined at creating stability, but fulfillment matters too. Align resources with your values so that decisions bring both peace and empowerment. Abundance grows when you appreciate what you already have. Today's clarity strengthens your financial foundation and boosts confidence in your path forward. Gratitude and wisdom together create prosperity.

Affirmation & Gratitude

I am grateful for financial wisdom and stability, trusting aligned choices bring both security and fulfillment.

Capricorn
20 September 2026

Communication is highlighted today. Important conversations may arise, offering clarity or new direction. Capricorn, your words carry influence—speak with intention and empathy. Listening carefully will be just as important as expressing yourself. Writing or teaching may also feel impactful now. The stars encourage you to blend reason with compassion, ensuring your message resonates. Today, dialogue builds bridges and opens doors that advance your journey.

Affirmation & Gratitude

I am grateful for the clarity and strength of my words, trusting communication builds connection and progress.

Capricorn
21 September 2026

Home and family life come into focus. Capricorn, you may feel called to nurture your sanctuary or strengthen bonds with loved ones. The stars remind you that your ambitions thrive when your roots are strong. Small gestures—repairing, organizing, or heartfelt connection—create harmony. By tending to your personal foundation, you fuel your broader goals. Today is about creating peace where it matters most—your heart and home.

Affirmation & Gratitude

I am grateful for the peace and strength of my home and family, trusting harmony here supports all I pursue.

Capricorn
22 September 2026

Creativity, romance, and joy are emphasized today. The stars encourage you to step into hobbies, playful expression, or heartfelt connections. Capricorn, responsibilities often dominate your schedule, but joy is not a distraction—it's nourishment for your soul. By allowing yourself to laugh, create, or embrace love, you restore balance. Inspiration sparked through fun may later shape your ambitions. Today, celebrate life's lighter side—it strengthens you for the challenges ahead.

Affirmation & Gratitude

I am grateful for joy, romance, and creativity, trusting play nourishes my spirit and inspires resilience.

Capricorn
23 September 2026

Work, health, and daily routines are highlighted. Capricorn, you may feel prompted to refine systems or introduce healthier habits. The stars encourage small but consistent changes that create lasting strength. Avoid pushing for perfection; instead, focus on sustainability. Your discipline makes you excellent at maintaining supportive routines, but balance is essential. Today, progress comes from mindful adjustments that honor both productivity and self-care.

Affirmation & Gratitude

I am grateful for supportive routines that bring balance, health, and strength, trusting small steps create lasting progress.

Capricorn
24 September 2026

Relationships take the spotlight. The stars encourage compromise, understanding, and emotional openness. Capricorn, your steadiness offers security, but vulnerability creates intimacy. Today is about finding harmony by listening to others while also expressing your needs. A heartfelt conversation could resolve misunderstandings or deepen trust. By balancing strength with softness, you create healthier, more resilient bonds. Partnerships thrive when both voices are honored.

Affirmation & Gratitude

I am grateful for the love and respect in my relationships, trusting openness strengthens connection and harmony.

Capricorn
25 September 2026

Shared resources, financial matters, or emotional bonds may rise to the surface. Transparency is essential. Capricorn, your grounded wisdom equips you to handle sensitive issues with fairness. Avoid letting assumptions complicate matters—clarity now prevents bigger challenges later. Emotional honesty is also highlighted: facing fears about trust or control empowers you. By confronting these dynamics directly, you build stronger foundations in both finances and relationships.

Affirmation & Gratitude

I am grateful for clarity and fairness in shared matters, trusting honesty builds stability and peace.

Capricorn
26 September 2026

Growth and exploration are emphasized. You may feel inspired to learn, travel, or connect with new perspectives. Capricorn, while structure supports you, the stars remind you that wisdom often comes from unfamiliar experiences. Stepping outside your comfort zone today enriches your path and sparks ideas that shape future ambitions. By welcoming curiosity, you invite wisdom that strengthens both your inner and outer worlds.

Affirmation & Gratitude

I am grateful for opportunities to expand my horizons, trusting curiosity leads me toward wisdom and growth.

Capricorn
27 September 2026

Career and reputation rise to the forefront. Recognition may arrive, or increased responsibilities could test your patience. Capricorn, your persistence and reliability are admired, but true leadership blends humility with authority. Today is a chance to refine ambitions to ensure they align with your deeper values. Success rooted in authenticity lasts longer than success built on appearances. Lead by example—your consistency inspires trust.

Affirmation & Gratitude

I am grateful for recognition of my persistence and integrity, trusting patience and authenticity create lasting success.

Capricorn
28 September 2026

Friendships and community connections are spotlighted. The stars encourage collaboration and shared vision. Capricorn, independence is your strength, but today reminds you of the power of teamwork. A friend may inspire you or provide guidance that sparks momentum. Cherish the relationships that uplift you—they are part of your foundation for resilience and progress. Connection strengthens both spirit and ambition.

Affirmation & Gratitude

I am grateful for supportive friendships and communities, trusting shared energy multiplies opportunities and joy.

Capricorn
29 September 2026

Solitude and reflection are important today. The stars remind you that rest restores clarity and strength. Capricorn, your drive often keeps you focused on external achievements, but inner alignment is equally important. By pausing, you create space for intuition to speak. Dreams or quiet insights may guide your next steps. Stillness today is not wasted—it prepares you for stronger forward strides.

Affirmation & Gratitude

I am grateful for peaceful moments of rest, trusting reflection restores clarity and energy.

Capricorn
30 September 2026

The Sun highlights your individuality and self-expression. Capricorn, today is about living authentically and embracing your true voice. By standing in your truth, you attract opportunities that align with your path. Your steady confidence inspires others, encouraging them to live authentically too. The stars remind you that your uniqueness is your strength—share it boldly. Today, shine without hesitation.

Affirmation & Gratitude

I am grateful for the courage to live authentically, trusting my truth attracts the right people and opportunities.

October 2026

Capricorn
01 October 2026

Finances and self-worth rise to the forefront. You may feel the urge to review money matters, savings, or investments. Capricorn, you're excellent at creating stability, but the stars encourage you to also consider how your financial decisions align with your deeper values. Security is essential, but fulfillment is just as important. Today, abundance is measured not only by what you earn, but also by how much gratitude you hold for what you already have.

Affirmation & Gratitude

I am grateful for financial wisdom and stability, trusting aligned choices create both security and fulfillment.

Capricorn
02 October 2026

Communication is emphasized today. Conversations may bring clarity, reveal opportunities, or highlight misunderstandings that need resolution. Capricorn, your words carry influence—use them with patience and intention. Listening deeply will provide as much value as speaking. This is also a strong day for writing, teaching, or sharing your insights publicly. The stars remind you that when reason is balanced with empathy, your message resonates far and wide.

Affirmation & Gratitude

I am grateful for the clarity and strength of my words, trusting communication builds trust and growth.

Capricorn
03 October 2026

Home and family life take center stage. You may feel drawn to tend to your sanctuary or strengthen bonds with loved ones. Capricorn, peace at home fortifies your ambitions in the wider world. Small gestures—sharing a meal, repairing your space, or honest conversations—create stability. The stars remind you that harmony in your private life lays the foundation for everything you build. Today, nurture your roots—they hold your greatest strength.

Affirmation & Gratitude

I am grateful for the peace of my home and family, trusting harmony here supports all that I pursue.

Capricorn
04 October 2026

Creativity, romance, and joy are emphasized. The stars encourage you to embrace hobbies, play, or heartfelt connection. Capricorn, you often prioritize responsibilities, but today reminds you that delight is not indulgent—it's restorative. By leaning into laughter, art, or love, you refuel your spirit and open yourself to inspiration. Fun today may spark motivation for future ambitions. Celebrate joy—it makes you stronger, not weaker.

Affirmation & Gratitude

I am grateful for joy, romance, and creativity, trusting play nourishes my spirit and sparks inspiration.

Capricorn
05 October 2026

Work, health, and routines are highlighted. Capricorn, you may feel called to refine your systems, build supportive habits, or tackle overdue responsibilities. The stars remind you that balance creates resilience—pushing too hard leads to burnout. Focus on sustainability, not perfection. Even one mindful adjustment today could ripple into long-term stability. Your discipline is your strength, but care for yourself is equally important. Today, align productivity with well-being.

Affirmation & Gratitude

I am grateful for supportive routines that nurture balance, health, and strength, trusting small steps create lasting results.

Capricorn
06 October 2026

Relationships are spotlighted today. The stars encourage compromise, empathy, and open communication. Capricorn, your steadiness creates security, but intimacy grows through vulnerability. A heartfelt conversation could bring healing or deepen trust. Healthy bonds thrive when both voices are valued and respected. By balancing strength with softness, you strengthen your connections. Today is a reminder that love and support are as essential as ambition.

Affirmation & Gratitude

I am grateful for the love and respect in my relationships, trusting openness and empathy create harmony and strength.

Capricorn
07 October 2026

Shared resources and emotional commitments may surface. Financial matters or trust issues could call for your attention. Capricorn, your grounded wisdom allows you to stabilize these situations with fairness. The stars encourage transparency—clarity now prevents future complications. Emotional honesty is equally important—acknowledging vulnerabilities frees you from their weight. By facing matters directly, you create stronger, healthier foundations. Today, courage and honesty transform tension into trust.

Affirmation & Gratitude

I am grateful for clarity and fairness in shared matters, trusting honesty builds stability and peace.

Capricorn
08 October 2026

Growth and exploration are highlighted. You may feel drawn to study, travel, or immerse yourself in a new perspective. Capricorn, while routine brings comfort, the stars encourage you to step outside your comfort zone. Fresh ideas and experiences today can plant seeds that shape your future direction. Wisdom is often found where you least expect it. Curiosity now becomes a catalyst for meaningful transformation and long-term progress.

Affirmation & Gratitude

I am grateful for opportunities to expand my horizons, trusting curiosity and openness lead me toward wisdom and growth.

Capricorn
09 October 2026

Career and reputation rise into focus. Recognition for your efforts may arrive, or you may be asked to shoulder greater responsibility. Capricorn, your persistence and discipline are admired, but the stars remind you to pair authority with humility. Success built steadily is stronger than quick wins. Today is about aligning ambition with authenticity, ensuring your goals reflect both purpose and integrity. Your steady example inspires trust and respect.

Affirmation & Gratitude

I am grateful for recognition of my persistence and integrity, trusting patience and authenticity create lasting success.

Capricorn
10 October 2026

Friendships and communities are spotlighted today. The stars encourage collaboration, teamwork, and connection. Capricorn, your independence is admirable, but collective energy magnifies possibility. A friend or colleague may offer advice or encouragement that sparks inspiration. Leaning into your circle now provides support and joy. Remember, success is sweeter when shared, and bonds nurtured today become part of your strength tomorrow. Connection is your anchor and your uplift.

Affirmation & Gratitude

I am grateful for supportive friendships and communities, trusting shared energy multiplies opportunity and joy.

Capricorn
11 October 2026

Solitude and reflection are essential. Capricorn, you may feel the need to retreat from external demands to recharge and reconnect with your inner compass. The stars remind you that stillness is not inactivity—it is nourishment for clarity. Pay attention to subtle messages in dreams or intuition; they may reveal guidance for the road ahead. By honoring rest today, you restore strength and focus for future achievements.

Affirmation & Gratitude

I am grateful for peaceful moments of rest, trusting reflection restores clarity and strength.

Capricorn
12 October 2026

The Sun illuminates your individuality and self-expression. Capricorn, today is about embracing your authentic voice and showcasing your talents unapologetically. By aligning with your truth, you attract the right opportunities. Your grounded confidence inspires others, encouraging them to live authentically too. The stars remind you that uniqueness is not a weakness—it's your greatest strength. Today is a call to shine boldly, without fear or hesitation.

Affirmation & Gratitude

I am grateful for the courage to live authentically, trusting my truth attracts aligned opportunities.

Capricorn
13 October 2026

Finances and self-worth take the spotlight today. The stars encourage you to reassess money habits and align them with your deeper values. Capricorn, your discipline helps you create stability, but fulfillment matters as much as security. Gratitude for what you already have expands abundance. Today, clear financial decisions will build both confidence and peace. Align money with meaning and you'll feel truly prosperous.

Affirmation & Gratitude

I am grateful for financial wisdom and stability, trusting aligned choices create both security and fulfillment.

Capricorn
14 October 2026

Communication is emphasized. Conversations may bring clarity, healing, or new opportunities. Capricorn, your words carry weight—use them with patience and empathy. Listening is equally important; insight may come from unexpected sources. This is also an excellent day for writing, teaching, or presenting. When reason is balanced with compassion, your message resonates strongly. Today, dialogue becomes a tool for progress, understanding, and connection.

Affirmation & Gratitude

I am grateful for the clarity and influence of my words, trusting communication builds bridges of trust and opportunity.

Capricorn
15 October 2026

Home and family life are emphasized today. You may feel the need to strengthen bonds, resolve tensions, or bring peace to your environment. Capricorn, your ambitions thrive when your roots are secure, and the stars remind you that small acts of care—organizing your space, cooking a meal, or simply offering time to loved ones—create harmony. By grounding yourself in your sanctuary, you renew energy for your wider goals. Peace at home is power everywhere.

Affirmation & Gratitude

I am grateful for the peace of my home and family, trusting harmony here supports everything I build.

Capricorn
16 October 2026

Creativity, romance, and joy take center stage. The stars encourage you to lean into hobbies, play, or heartfelt connection. Capricorn, you often prioritize responsibility, but joy is nourishment for your spirit. By allowing yourself to laugh, create, and love, you restore balance. Inspiration found in fun may ripple into professional growth later. Today, celebrate the lighter side of life—it strengthens your resilience and sparks your inner fire.

Affirmation & Gratitude

I am grateful for joy, romance, and creativity, trusting play nourishes my spirit and sparks inspiration.

Capricorn
17 October 2026

Work, health, and routines are spotlighted. You may feel called to refine habits, restructure systems, or improve well-being. Capricorn, your discipline makes you excellent at maintaining consistency, but the stars remind you to prioritize balance as well as productivity. Even small changes today can create long-term strength. Progress is found in sustainable practices, not overexertion. Focus on aligning your daily life with habits that truly support your long-term vision.

Affirmation & Gratitude

I am grateful for supportive routines that nurture health, strength, and balance, trusting steady steps create lasting results.

Capricorn
18 October 2026

Relationships take the spotlight. The stars highlight compromise, understanding, and honest conversation. Capricorn, your reliability creates stability, but intimacy deepens when you allow vulnerability. Today is about balancing your needs with those of others, ensuring both sides feel valued. A heartfelt dialogue could strengthen bonds or resolve lingering issues. By leaning into empathy and openness, you create trust and harmony that lasts. Love thrives where respect and honesty flow.

Affirmation & Gratitude

I am grateful for love and respect in my relationships, trusting openness creates stronger bonds.

Capricorn
19 October 2026

Shared resources, finances, or emotional bonds may surface today. Transparency is essential—uncertainty or avoidance only creates tension. Capricorn, your practical wisdom equips you to bring stability and fairness. The stars encourage you to face matters directly, whether involving money, agreements, or trust. Emotional honesty is just as important as practical clarity. By addressing these themes with courage, you build resilience and strengthen bonds rooted in fairness and security.

Affirmation & Gratitude
I am grateful for clarity and fairness in shared matters, trusting honesty builds stability and peace.

Capricorn
20 October 2026

Growth and exploration are emphasized. You may feel called to study, travel, or adopt a new philosophy. Capricorn, while structure grounds you, today the stars remind you that wisdom often comes from unfamiliar paths. By staying curious, you invite inspiration and new opportunities. A fresh perspective could plant seeds that guide your ambitions forward. Today is about stretching beyond comfort zones and welcoming change as a catalyst for growth.

Affirmation & Gratitude

I am grateful for opportunities to expand my horizons, trusting curiosity leads me toward wisdom and growth.

Capricorn
21 October 2026

Career and public reputation take the spotlight. Recognition may arrive, or greater responsibilities may be assigned. Capricorn, your persistence and integrity are admired, but true leadership comes from humility as well as authority. The stars encourage you to refine your ambitions to ensure they align with your authentic values. Success built on authenticity endures. By leading through consistency and fairness, you inspire others to trust your path.

Affirmation & Gratitude

I am grateful for recognition of my persistence and integrity, trusting patience and authenticity create lasting success.

Capricorn
22 October 2026

Friendships and community ties are spotlighted today. The stars encourage collaboration, shared vision, and connection. Capricorn, independence fuels your strength, but today reminds you that connection multiplies possibility. A friend's support or advice could spark a breakthrough. Networking may open doors you hadn't expected. By investing in these bonds, you not only gain joy but also resilience. Success feels lighter when shared. Today, treasure the people who uplift and inspire you.

Affirmation & Gratitude

I am grateful for supportive friendships and communities, trusting shared vision multiplies opportunity and joy.

Capricorn
23 October 2026

Solitude and reflection are essential. The stars remind you that stillness creates clarity. Capricorn, you may feel the urge to withdraw from the noise and reconnect with yourself. Pay attention to dreams, intuition, or subtle signs—they carry guidance for your next steps. By slowing down, you create room for renewal. Rest is not weakness—it is fuel for tomorrow's progress. Today, trust silence as a powerful teacher.

Affirmation & Gratitude

I am grateful for peaceful moments of rest, trusting reflection restores my strength and clarity.

Capricorn
24 October 2026

The Sun illuminates your individuality and self-expression. Capricorn, today is about living authentically and owning your truth. By embracing your uniqueness, you inspire others to do the same. The stars encourage you to share talents, voice, or vision boldly—without apology. Your grounded confidence carries weight, drawing the right people and opportunities. Today is a reminder that authenticity attracts alignment. Shine proudly; your light guides more than just yourself.

Affirmation & Gratitude

I am grateful for the courage to live authentically, trusting my truth attracts aligned opportunities.

Capricorn
25 October 2026

Finances and self-worth come into focus. You may feel urged to reevaluate money habits or consider how resources align with your values. Capricorn, your discipline ensures stability, but abundance also means enjoying what you already have. The stars remind you to balance security with fulfillment. Today is about empowerment—making choices that create peace of mind while reflecting purpose. Clarity now builds both confidence and financial stability for the long term.

Affirmation & Gratitude

I am grateful for financial wisdom and stability, trusting aligned choices create abundance and confidence.

Capricorn
26 October 2026

Communication is emphasized. Important conversations may arise, offering clarity or new direction. Capricorn, your words carry influence—use them thoughtfully and listen carefully. Misunderstandings can be resolved with patience. This is also a favorable time for writing, teaching, or sharing your perspective publicly. The stars remind you that when logic is balanced with compassion, your message resonates. Today, dialogue becomes a powerful tool for progress, healing, and connection.

Affirmation & Gratitude

I am grateful for the clarity and influence of my words, trusting communication builds bridges of trust and understanding.

Capricorn
27 October 2026

Home and family matters are highlighted. Capricorn, you may feel called to create peace in your personal sanctuary or resolve family dynamics. The stars encourage you to strengthen your foundation—your ambitions thrive when your roots feel secure. Whether through small acts of care or deeper conversations, focus on harmony at home. Nurturing your sanctuary today provides strength for all you pursue in the wider world.

Affirmation & Gratitude

I am grateful for the peace of my home and family, trusting strong roots support everything I build.

Capricorn
28 October 2026

Creativity, romance, and joy take the spotlight. The stars encourage playful expression, hobbies, or heartfelt connection. Capricorn, you often prioritize duty, but today is about celebrating delight as nourishment. Fun restores your spirit and sparks inspiration. Laughter and love fuel resilience, making you stronger for challenges ahead. By embracing life's lighter side, you invite balance and fulfillment into your journey. Today, joy itself becomes an act of strength.

Affirmation & Gratitude

I am grateful for joy, romance, and creativity, trusting play nourishes my spirit and sparks inspiration.

Capricorn
29 October 2026

Work, health, and daily routines are in focus. Capricorn, you may feel prompted to refine systems or adopt healthier habits. The stars encourage consistency over extremes—sustainability creates resilience. Focus on small steps that align productivity with self-care. Your discipline ensures results, but balance protects your energy. Today, progress is found in mindful adjustments that support both well-being and ambition.

Affirmation & Gratitude

I am grateful for supportive routines that nurture health, balance, and strength, trusting small steps create lasting results.

Capricorn
30 October 2026

Relationships are emphasized. The stars encourage compromise, openness, and empathy. Capricorn, your steadiness provides reassurance, but intimacy grows when you allow vulnerability. A heartfelt conversation today could transform a bond—healing rifts or deepening closeness. Healthy partnerships thrive on trust and respect. Today is about strengthening your connections by balancing strength with softness. Love requires not only commitment but also openness.

Affirmation & Gratitude

I am grateful for love and respect in my relationships, trusting openness creates harmony and trust.

Capricorn
31 October 2026

Shared resources and emotional bonds take center stage. Issues involving finances, agreements, or trust may need attention. Capricorn, your grounded wisdom equips you to handle these matters fairly. Transparency prevents complications, while emotional honesty strengthens bonds. The stars encourage you to face issues directly—courage today builds security tomorrow. By embracing clarity, you transform tension into trust and stability. This is a day to create balance in shared commitments.

Affirmation & Gratitude

I am grateful for clarity and fairness in shared matters, trusting honesty builds stability and peace.

November 2026

Capricorn
01 November 2026

Growth and exploration are emphasized today. You may feel inspired to study, travel, or immerse yourself in a new philosophy. Capricorn, your disciplined mind benefits from stepping outside familiar routines. The stars encourage you to welcome fresh perspectives—they will expand your understanding of yourself and the world. Curiosity today is a seed for long-term progress. Trust that even small explorations bring wisdom that strengthens your ambitions and your spirit.

Affirmation & Gratitude

I am grateful for opportunities to expand my horizons, trusting curiosity leads me toward wisdom and long-term growth.

Capricorn
02 November 2026

Career and reputation rise into focus. Recognition for your steady efforts may arrive, or greater responsibility may be offered. Capricorn, your persistence and integrity are admired, but the stars remind you that true leadership balances authority with humility. Today is an excellent time to refine ambitions and align them with your values. By leading through example, you inspire trust and respect. Legacy is built through consistent actions, not fleeting applause.

Affirmation & Gratitude

I am grateful for recognition of my persistence and integrity, trusting patience and authenticity create lasting success.

Capricorn
03 November 2026

Friendships and communities are spotlighted. The stars encourage collaboration and collective energy. Capricorn, your independence is admirable, but teamwork expands your possibilities. A friend's encouragement or advice may spark momentum. Lean into your circle for inspiration and support. Today is about honoring the people who uplift you and recognizing that shared vision multiplies potential. Community nurtures both joy and resilience, helping you stay strong on your path.

Affirmation & Gratitude

I am grateful for supportive friendships and communities, trusting shared energy multiplies opportunities and joy.

Capricorn
04 November 2026

Solitude and reflection are essential. Capricorn, you may feel the urge to step away from external demands and recharge. The stars remind you that rest is not laziness—it is renewal. Dreams or intuition may offer valuable guidance if you listen. Stillness today restores clarity and strength, preparing you for the next chapter. By reconnecting with your inner voice, you create alignment and direction. Silence is not empty—it's full of answers.

Affirmation & Gratitude

I am grateful for peaceful moments of rest, trusting reflection restores my strength and clarity.

Capricorn
05 November 2026

The Sun illuminates your individuality and personal expression. Capricorn, today is about owning your truth and sharing it without apology. When you live authentically, you attract opportunities that align with your path. Your steady confidence inspires others to honor themselves as well. The stars remind you that your uniqueness is your power. Today, step forward boldly—your presence carries influence, and your authenticity is your gift to the world.

Affirmation & Gratitude

I am grateful for the courage to live authentically, trusting my truth attracts the right people and opportunities.

Capricorn
06 November 2026

Finances and self-worth are spotlighted. You may feel called to review money matters, savings, or investments. Capricorn, your discipline creates stability, but the stars remind you that fulfillment is as important as security. Aligning financial decisions with your values ensures both peace and empowerment. Gratitude for what you already have expands abundance. Today is about building confidence by making clear, purposeful choices that reflect both practicality and meaning.

Affirmation & Gratitude

I am grateful for financial wisdom and stability, trusting aligned choices create both security and fulfillment.

Capricorn
07 November 2026

Communication is emphasized today. Conversations may carry greater significance, offering clarity or resolving tension. Capricorn, your words have influence—use them with intention and compassion. Listening will be just as powerful as speaking. This is also a favorable day for writing, teaching, or sharing your voice publicly. The stars remind you that when logic blends with empathy, your message resonates widely. Authentic dialogue today becomes a tool for healing and progress.

Affirmation & Gratitude

I am grateful for the clarity and strength of my words, trusting communication builds bridges of trust and growth.

Capricorn
08 November 2026

Home and family life are in focus. You may feel the need to strengthen your sanctuary, repair relationships, or create more comfort in your environment. Capricorn, your ambitions thrive when your roots are steady. The stars encourage you to pay attention to small details at home that bring peace and stability—whether that's tidying, cooking, or heartfelt connection. Harmony here supports everything else you build. Today is about nurturing the foundations that carry you forward.

Affirmation & Gratitude

I am grateful for the peace of my home and family, trusting harmony here supports all I build.

Capricorn
09 November 2026

Creativity, romance, and joy are emphasized. The stars encourage you to lean into play, expression, or love. Capricorn, you often prioritize duty, but today is about celebrating delight. Fun restores your energy and sparks inspiration that can ripple into your professional life later. By allowing yourself to embrace joy, you strengthen resilience. Remember: play is not a distraction—it's fuel for the spirit and motivation for bigger dreams.

Affirmation & Gratitude

I am grateful for joy, romance, and creativity, trusting play nourishes my spirit and sparks inspiration.

Capricorn
10 November 2026

Work, health, and routines are spotlighted. Capricorn, your discipline ensures consistency, but the stars encourage you to evaluate whether your habits truly support your well-being. Today is about refining systems, reorganizing schedules, or adopting healthier practices. Even small adjustments bring long-term benefits. Balance is vital—burnout serves no one. By aligning productivity with self-care, you create resilience and stamina to carry you through ambitious goals. Sustainability is your focus today.

Affirmation & Gratitude

I am grateful for supportive routines that bring health, strength, and balance, trusting steady steps create lasting results.

Capricorn
11 November 2026

Relationships take the spotlight today. The stars highlight compromise, understanding, and open-hearted dialogue. Capricorn, your reliability creates security, but vulnerability builds intimacy. A meaningful conversation could heal a rift or bring deeper connection. Remember that true partnerships thrive when both sides feel valued. By balancing strength with softness, you create lasting harmony. Today is a reminder that love and respect are as essential to your journey as ambition.

Affirmation & Gratitude

I am grateful for the love and respect in my relationships, trusting openness creates deeper harmony and connection.

Capricorn
12 November 2026

Shared resources or emotional commitments may require your attention. Issues around money, agreements, or trust may arise. Capricorn, your grounded wisdom helps you navigate these matters fairly. The stars encourage you to be transparent—avoid secrecy or assumption. Emotional honesty also matters; acknowledging vulnerability brings freedom and trust. By facing issues directly, you prevent future complications and strengthen foundations. Today, courage and fairness create balance in shared matters.

Affirmation & Gratitude

I am grateful for clarity and fairness in shared matters, trusting honesty builds stability and trust.

Capricorn
13 November 2026

Growth and exploration are emphasized. The stars encourage you to step beyond your usual boundaries, whether through study, travel, or fresh perspectives. Capricorn, you thrive on structure, but wisdom often comes from unfamiliar paths. Curiosity today may spark inspiration that influences long-term goals. By embracing new ideas, you enrich both your inner and outer journey. Expansion strengthens your vision and keeps your ambitions aligned with purpose.

Affirmation & Gratitude

I am grateful for opportunities to expand my horizons, trusting curiosity and openness lead me toward wisdom and growth.

Capricorn
14 November 2026

Career and reputation are spotlighted. Recognition for your persistence may arrive, or new responsibilities may surface. Capricorn, your reliability is admired, but the stars remind you that true success is measured by integrity as well as achievement. Today is a good time to refine ambitions, ensuring they reflect your deeper values. By leading through consistency and authenticity, you inspire respect. Success built on patience endures far longer than quick wins.

Affirmation & Gratitude

I am grateful for recognition of my persistence and integrity, trusting patience and authenticity create lasting success.

Capricorn
15 November 2026

Friendships and community connections are emphasized today. Capricorn, your independence is admirable, but the stars encourage you to lean into collective energy. A friend may inspire you or offer encouragement that sparks motivation. Teamwork magnifies opportunities you may not access alone. By cherishing your support system, you strengthen both your joy and resilience. Today is about appreciating the people who walk beside you—they are part of your success story too.

Affirmation & Gratitude

I am grateful for supportive friendships and communities, trusting shared vision and encouragement multiply opportunity and joy.

Capricorn
16 November 2026

Solitude and reflection are essential. Capricorn, you may feel the urge to step back from external demands and recharge. The stars remind you that stillness restores clarity and energy. Intuition may offer important insights if you listen carefully. By honoring your need for rest today, you create space for wisdom and strength to emerge. Renewal isn't retreat—it's preparation for the road ahead. Silence is your ally now.

Affirmation & Gratitude

I am grateful for peaceful moments of rest, trusting stillness restores clarity, energy, and wisdom.

Capricorn
17 November 2026

The Sun illuminates your individuality and self-expression. Capricorn, today is about embracing your truth and sharing it boldly. When you live authentically, you naturally attract opportunities aligned with your purpose. Your quiet confidence inspires others to step into their truth as well. The stars encourage you to stop dimming your light—shine unapologetically. Today is a reminder that authenticity is your most powerful asset.

Affirmation & Gratitude

I am grateful for the courage to live authentically, trusting my truth attracts aligned people and opportunities.

Capricorn
18 November 2026

Finances and self-worth are spotlighted. Capricorn, you may feel called to review budgets, income, or investments. The stars remind you that stability is important, but fulfillment is equally vital. Aligning money decisions with your deeper values creates empowerment and peace. Gratitude for what you already have allows abundance to expand. Today, clarity around your finances will also strengthen your sense of confidence and self-worth moving forward.

Affirmation & Gratitude

I am grateful for financial wisdom and stability, trusting aligned choices create both security and fulfillment.

Capricorn
19 November 2026

Communication is emphasized. Conversations may bring clarity, resolve misunderstandings, or spark new opportunities. Capricorn, your words carry influence—use them with patience and empathy. Listening is equally important—wisdom may come from unexpected voices. This is also an excellent day for writing or sharing your insights publicly. When reason and compassion work together, your message resonates far and wide. Today is about building bridges through honest dialogue.

Affirmation & Gratitude

I am grateful for the clarity and influence of my words, trusting communication builds trust and growth.

Capricorn
20 November 2026

Home and family life take priority. Capricorn, your ambitions soar higher when your roots are steady. The stars encourage you to create harmony in your personal space—whether through physical improvements, heartfelt conversation, or simply quality time with loved ones. Peace within your sanctuary fuels confidence and focus in your outer world. Today is about nurturing the foundation that supports all your dreams.

Affirmation & Gratitude

I am grateful for the peace of my home and family, trusting harmony here strengthens all I pursue.

Capricorn
21 November 2026

Creativity, romance, and joy take center stage. Capricorn, the stars encourage you to embrace hobbies, love, or playful expression. Responsibilities may weigh on you, but today is about restoring balance through delight. Fun isn't frivolous—it replenishes your spirit and sparks inspiration that can flow into your ambitions later. By leaning into joy, you strengthen both resilience and fulfillment. Today is about celebrating life's beauty with openness and laughter.

Affirmation & Gratitude
I am grateful for joy, romance, and creativity, trusting play nourishes my spirit and inspires resilience.

Capricorn
22 November 2026

Work, health, and routines are spotlighted. Capricorn, you may feel called to review daily habits, adjust responsibilities, or introduce healthier practices. The stars encourage sustainability over perfection—progress grows from small, consistent changes. Balance is vital: don't push to exhaustion. Today is about creating a rhythm that supports both productivity and well-being. When your body and mind are cared for, your ambitions flourish more easily and with greater longevity.

Affirmation & Gratitude

I am grateful for supportive routines that nurture balance, strength, and health, trusting steady steps create lasting results.

Capricorn
23 November 2026

Relationships are highlighted today. The stars encourage empathy, compromise, and vulnerability. Capricorn, your steadiness builds security, but intimacy deepens when you open your heart. A heartfelt conversation could heal rifts or strengthen bonds. Partnerships thrive when both voices are respected and valued. By leaning into openness, you create space for harmony and deeper connection. Today is about nurturing love with honesty and patience—it is as vital as ambition.

Affirmation & Gratitude

I am grateful for love and respect in my relationships, trusting openness builds harmony and deeper connection.

Capricorn
24 November 2026

Shared resources, financial matters, or emotional bonds may surface. Capricorn, the stars encourage honesty and fairness. Avoid avoidance—clarity prevents misunderstandings. Your practical wisdom equips you to bring balance to sensitive situations. This is also a powerful day for emotional honesty—facing fears about trust or control strengthens resilience. By addressing matters directly, you create stability for the long term. Courage today lays foundations for security tomorrow.

Affirmation & Gratitude

I am grateful for clarity and fairness in shared matters, trusting honesty builds stability and peace.

Capricorn
25 November 2026

Growth and exploration are emphasized. The stars encourage you to step into new perspectives through study, travel, or fresh conversations. Capricorn, while structure comforts you, wisdom is often found outside familiar territory. Inspiration today may guide long-term goals. By staying open and curious, you expand your worldview and enrich both your ambitions and spirit. Embrace opportunities that stretch your comfort zone —they carry seeds for transformation.

Affirmation & Gratitude

I am grateful for opportunities to expand my horizons, trusting curiosity and openness lead me to wisdom and growth.

Capricorn
26 November 2026

Career and reputation take the spotlight. Capricorn, your persistence and reliability may be recognized today, or greater responsibilities may be offered. The stars remind you to align ambitions with authenticity. Success built on integrity lasts longer than quick wins. Lead by example and inspire through consistency. By refining your goals to reflect deeper purpose, you create a legacy that will endure.

Affirmation & Gratitude

I am grateful for recognition of my persistence and integrity, trusting patience and authenticity create lasting success.

Capricorn
27 November 2026

Friendships and communities are emphasized. The stars encourage collaboration and support. Capricorn, independence defines you, but shared vision multiplies opportunity. A friend may offer advice or encouragement that sparks fresh direction. By cherishing your connections, you gain both joy and resilience. Today is about honoring the people who uplift you—they are part of your journey's strength. Together, possibilities expand further than you could achieve alone.

Affirmation & Gratitude

I am grateful for supportive friendships and communities, trusting shared energy multiplies opportunities and joy.

Capricorn
28 November 2026

Solitude and reflection are necessary. Capricorn, the stars remind you that stillness is just as important as effort. By stepping back, you reconnect with intuition and gain clarity for your next steps. Dreams, journaling, or meditation may provide powerful insights. Rest is not retreat—it is renewal. Today, give yourself permission to pause. By restoring your spirit now, you prepare yourself for stronger forward momentum.

Affirmation & Gratitude

I am grateful for peaceful moments of rest, trusting reflection restores clarity, wisdom, and strength.

Capricorn
29 November 2026

The Sun highlights your individuality and self-expression. Capricorn, today is about embracing authenticity and shining unapologetically. When you stand firmly in your truth, you draw aligned opportunities and inspire others to do the same. The stars remind you that your uniqueness is your power. Step boldly into your story today—own it without hesitation. Authenticity is your greatest magnet for success and fulfillment.

Affirmation & Gratitude

I am grateful for the courage to live authentically, trusting my truth attracts aligned opportunities and connections.

Capricorn
30 November 2026

Finances and self-worth rise into focus. Capricorn, you may feel urged to review spending, savings, or investments. The stars encourage balance—security is important, but fulfillment is just as vital. Abundance grows when you align money with values and appreciate what you already have. Today, clear financial choices create both confidence and peace of mind. Prosperity flows most strongly when it serves your true purpose.

Affirmation & Gratitude

I am grateful for financial wisdom and stability, trusting aligned choices create both abundance and peace.

December 2026

Capricorn
01 December 2026

Communication is emphasized today. The stars highlight conversations, negotiations, or the exchange of ideas that could shift your perspective. Capricorn, your grounded words carry influence, but empathy gives them true power. Listening carefully will reveal as much as speaking. This is also a strong day for writing, teaching, or presenting. Honest dialogue clears misunderstandings and builds new opportunities. By balancing reason with compassion, you create connection and trust that ripple outward.

Affirmation & Gratitude

I am grateful for the clarity and strength of my words, trusting communication builds bridges of trust and growth.

Capricorn
02 December 2026

Home and family life are spotlighted. Capricorn, you may feel drawn to nurture your space, resolve household matters, or simply enjoy time with loved ones. The stars remind you that peace in your sanctuary creates stability for everything else you build. Even small gestures—cleaning, sharing a meal, or an honest conversation—bring harmony. Today, grounding yourself at home replenishes your strength for the wider world. Roots give wings to your ambitions.

Affirmation & Gratitude

I am grateful for the peace of my home and family, trusting harmony here strengthens all that I pursue.

Capricorn
03 December 2026

Creativity, romance, and joy take center stage. The stars encourage you to embrace hobbies, laughter, or love. Capricorn, while duty often calls, today's message is to celebrate life's lighter side. Fun restores your spirit, balances your perspective, and sparks inspiration that may flow into professional growth later. Joy is not indulgence—it's essential fuel for your ambitions. By leaning into delight, you cultivate resilience and a renewed sense of purpose.

Affirmation & Gratitude

I am grateful for joy, romance, and creativity, trusting play nourishes my spirit and sparks inspiration.

Capricorn
04 December 2026

Work, health, and routines are emphasized. Capricorn, your discipline supports consistency, but today the stars encourage you to ensure your systems also support well-being. Small, sustainable changes are more powerful than drastic shifts. Avoid burnout—productivity thrives when self-care is part of the plan. Today is about balance: creating habits that nurture both body and mind while sustaining your ambitious goals. Progress grows from steady, thoughtful steps.

Affirmation & Gratitude

I am grateful for supportive routines that bring balance, health, and strength, trusting steady steps create lasting results.

Capricorn
05 December 2026

Relationships take the spotlight. The stars encourage compromise, patience, and vulnerability. Capricorn, your steadiness builds trust, but intimacy deepens when you open your heart. Honest conversations today could heal misunderstandings or deepen connection. Partnerships flourish when both voices are heard and valued. By balancing strength with softness, you create harmony. Today, focus on building bonds rooted in respect and love—they are just as vital as achievement.

Affirmation & Gratitude

I am grateful for love and respect in my relationships, trusting openness strengthens bonds and creates harmony.

Capricorn
06 December 2026

Shared resources and emotional commitments may surface. The stars encourage transparency—clarity now prevents future complications. Capricorn, your grounded wisdom equips you to stabilize sensitive matters fairly. This is also a day for emotional honesty. Facing fears around vulnerability or control will free you from unnecessary tension. Courage today transforms challenges into stability and trust. By addressing issues directly, you strengthen both your confidence and your connections.

Affirmation & Gratitude

I am grateful for clarity and fairness in shared matters, trusting honesty builds stability and peace.

Capricorn
07 December 2026

Growth and exploration are emphasized. Capricorn, you may feel inspired to learn, travel, or broaden your spiritual and intellectual horizons. The stars remind you that wisdom often comes from experiences outside familiar paths. By staying curious, you enrich both your inner journey and your external ambitions. Today's opportunities may plant seeds that guide your long-term goals. Be open—expansion today strengthens your path tomorrow.

Affirmation & Gratitude

I am grateful for opportunities to expand my horizons, trusting curiosity and openness lead me to wisdom and growth.

Capricorn
08 December 2026

Career and public reputation rise into focus today. Recognition may arrive, or new responsibilities may challenge you to step forward. Capricorn, your persistence and integrity are admired, but the stars remind you that humility strengthens leadership. True success is measured not only by achievement but by how authentically it reflects your values. Refine your goals now to ensure they align with your deeper purpose. Consistency, patience, and authenticity will secure lasting respect.

Affirmation & Gratitude

I am grateful for recognition of my persistence and integrity, trusting patience and authenticity create lasting success.

Capricorn
09 December 2026

Friendships and community ties are highlighted. The stars encourage collaboration and shared vision. Capricorn, your independence is a strength, but today reminds you that support from others multiplies opportunity. A friend's perspective may spark fresh inspiration or open doors you hadn't considered. Cherish the people who uplift you—they are part of your foundation for resilience and joy. Today is about honoring the bonds that keep you strong.

Affirmation & Gratitude

I am grateful for supportive friendships and communities, trusting shared vision multiplies opportunities and joy.

Capricorn
10 December 2026

Solitude and reflection are emphasized. Capricorn, you may feel the pull to step back from demands and recharge. The stars remind you that stillness is not wasted—it restores strength and clarity. Dreams, meditation, or journaling may reveal insights to guide your next steps. Today is about inner alignment: pausing now so that you can move forward with renewed focus. Silence holds wisdom—listen carefully.

Affirmation & Gratitude
I am grateful for peaceful moments of rest, trusting stillness restores clarity and strength.

Capricorn
11 December 2026

The Sun illuminates your individuality and self-expression. Capricorn, today encourages you to stand confidently in your truth. By embracing your uniqueness unapologetically, you attract opportunities aligned with your authentic self. Your steady confidence inspires others to live authentically too. The stars remind you that your story matters—share it boldly. Today is about shining as yourself, without hesitation or apology.

Affirmation & Gratitude

I am grateful for the courage to live authentically, trusting my truth attracts aligned opportunities.

Capricorn
12 December 2026

Finances and self-worth are spotlighted. Capricorn, the stars encourage you to review money decisions and ensure they align with your values. Security is important, but fulfillment matters just as much. Abundance grows when you appreciate what you already have. Today is about empowerment—building stability through clarity while also recognizing your worth beyond material success. By aligning resources with meaning, you create both prosperity and peace of mind.

Affirmation & Gratitude

I am grateful for financial wisdom and stability, trusting aligned choices create both abundance and confidence.

Capricorn
13 December 2026

Communication is emphasized. Conversations may bring clarity, resolve tension, or spark new opportunities. Capricorn, your words carry influence—use them with patience and empathy. Listening will be just as powerful as speaking. This is also a strong day for writing or teaching, as your perspective inspires trust. The stars remind you that dialogue builds bridges. Today, balance reason with compassion and you'll see breakthroughs in connection and progress.

Affirmation & Gratitude

I am grateful for the clarity and influence of my words, trusting communication builds trust and opportunity.

Capricorn
14 December 2026

Home and family life are in focus. Capricorn, peace within your sanctuary strengthens your confidence in the wider world. The stars encourage you to tend to your space, resolve domestic issues, or share meaningful moments with loved ones. Even small acts—reorganizing, repairing, or reconnecting—create harmony. By nurturing your roots, you fuel your ambitions. Today is about grounding yourself where love and security give you strength.

Affirmation & Gratitude

I am grateful for the peace of my home and family, trusting harmony here supports all I pursue.

Capricorn
15 December 2026

Creativity, romance, and joy are emphasized today. The stars encourage you to loosen your grip on duty and embrace play. Capricorn, responsibilities will always be there, but joy replenishes your spirit and sparks inspiration that may ripple into your ambitions. By allowing yourself to laugh, love, and create, you restore balance and strengthen resilience. Fun today is not wasted —it's fuel for tomorrow's progress. Celebrate delight—it's an important part of your path.

Affirmation & Gratitude

I am grateful for joy, romance, and creativity, trusting play nourishes my spirit and sparks inspiration.

Capricorn
16 December 2026

Work, health, and routines rise to focus. Capricorn, you may feel called to refine systems, build healthier habits, or reassess responsibilities. The stars encourage sustainability over perfection. Progress is made by steady, manageable steps rather than extremes. Align your schedule so that it supports both productivity and well-being. Today, consistency is more important than intensity—small, wise changes have long-lasting results. Caring for your body and mind ensures energy for bigger goals.

Affirmation & Gratitude

I am grateful for supportive routines that nurture health, balance, and strength, trusting steady steps create lasting resilience.

Capricorn
17 December 2026

Relationships are spotlighted today. The stars encourage compromise, empathy, and vulnerability. Capricorn, your steadiness builds trust, but openness builds intimacy. A meaningful conversation could heal tension or strengthen bonds. True connection comes when both sides feel heard and valued. By balancing strength with softness, you deepen your partnerships and create harmony. Today is about choosing love and understanding as much as ambition. Relationships flourish when nurtured with honesty and respect.

Affirmation & Gratitude

I am grateful for love and respect in my relationships, trusting openness creates harmony and connection.

Capricorn
18 December 2026

Shared resources and emotional commitments may need attention. The stars highlight trust, boundaries, and fairness. Capricorn, your grounded wisdom equips you to stabilize sensitive situations. Avoid assumptions—clarity now prevents future complications. Emotional honesty is equally important: acknowledging fears around vulnerability creates strength. By addressing matters directly, you foster trust and stability. Today, courage transforms potential conflict into an opportunity for deeper connection and mutual security.

Affirmation & Gratitude

I am grateful for clarity and fairness in shared matters, trusting honesty builds stability and trust.

Capricorn
19 December 2026

Growth and exploration are emphasized. The stars encourage you to welcome new experiences—study, travel, or philosophical reflection may expand your horizons. Capricorn, while structure anchors you, wisdom often comes from stepping into the unknown. Inspiration found today may shape your long-term goals. Curiosity isn't a distraction—it's part of your journey. Embrace the adventure of learning, and allow fresh perspectives to fuel both spirit and ambition.

Affirmation & Gratitude

I am grateful for opportunities to expand my horizons, trusting curiosity and openness lead me to wisdom and growth.

Capricorn
20 December 2026

Career and reputation rise into focus. Recognition may arrive, or responsibilities may weigh heavily. Capricorn, your persistence and integrity are noticed, but the stars remind you to pair ambition with humility. Today is an opportunity to refine goals so they reflect your deeper values. Lead with integrity—success built on authenticity lasts. By showing consistency and fairness, you inspire others to trust your leadership.

Affirmation & Gratitude

I am grateful for recognition of my persistence and integrity, trusting patience and authenticity create lasting success.

Capricorn
21 December 2026

Friendships and communities are spotlighted. Capricorn, the stars encourage collaboration and shared vision. Independence defines you, but teamwork multiplies opportunities. A friend may bring guidance or encouragement that sparks fresh ideas. By leaning into your support system, you gain inspiration and resilience. Community offers strength that you cannot always create alone. Today is about honoring the bonds that lift you higher and appreciating the joy they bring.

Affirmation & Gratitude

I am grateful for supportive friendships and communities, trusting shared vision multiplies opportunities and joy.

Capricorn
22 December 2026

Solitude and reflection are highlighted. Capricorn, with the year drawing to a close, the stars encourage you to pause and reconnect with your inner compass. Stillness brings clarity you cannot access in constant motion. Dreams, journaling, or meditation may provide guidance for your next cycle. Today is not about action but about realignment. Rest restores your strength, ensuring you enter the new year with focus and purpose. Honor silence—it is fertile with wisdom.

Affirmation & Gratitude

I am grateful for peaceful moments of rest, trusting reflection restores clarity, strength, and direction.

Capricorn
23 December 2026

The Sun illuminates your individuality and self-expression. Capricorn, today calls you to embrace authenticity and share it proudly. By standing in your truth, you attract opportunities aligned with your purpose. Your quiet confidence inspires others to embrace themselves fully. The stars remind you that uniqueness is power—it makes you magnetic. Today, shine without hesitation or fear. This is a day for honoring your story and owning your strength.

Affirmation & Gratitude

I am grateful for the courage to live authentically, trusting my truth attracts aligned opportunities.

Capricorn
24 December 2026

Finances and self-worth are spotlighted. As the holidays approach, you may be reminded of the balance between giving, saving, and enjoying. Capricorn, your discipline creates stability, but fulfillment comes from aligning money choices with your deeper values. Gratitude expands abundance, reminding you prosperity isn't just about material gain—it's also about confidence and peace. Today, wise financial reflection strengthens both stability and empowerment as you prepare for the new year ahead.

Affirmation & Gratitude

I am grateful for financial wisdom and stability, trusting aligned choices bring both security and peace.

Capricorn
25 December 2026

Communication is emphasized. The festive energy may bring heartfelt conversations, healing old misunderstandings, or deepening bonds. Capricorn, your words carry weight—speak with kindness and patience. Listening is just as important today; wisdom may come from the most unexpected places. This is also a day to share gratitude openly—your voice of appreciation may uplift others. The stars remind you that communication today builds joy and connection that lasts.

Affirmation & Gratitude

I am grateful for the clarity and warmth of my words, trusting communication builds harmony and connection.

Capricorn
26 December 2026

Home and family life take priority. The stars encourage you to embrace comfort and togetherness. Capricorn, your sanctuary is your strength—peace here creates stability everywhere else. Small gestures, whether laughter, meals, or simply presence, build memories that endure. Today, nurture the bonds closest to you; they are the heart of your foundation. By investing in harmony, you renew energy for future ambitions. Love at home is your true anchor.

Affirmation & Gratitude

I am grateful for the peace and love of my home and family, trusting harmony here supports all I pursue.

Capricorn
27 December 2026

Creativity, joy, and romance are highlighted. Capricorn, responsibilities may feel heavy, but the stars encourage you to embrace lightheartedness. Fun today is nourishment, not distraction. Hobbies, love, and laughter restore balance, helping you approach the future with renewed energy. Inspiration found through joy may ripple into your goals next year. By leaning into delight, you cultivate resilience and creativity. Today is about celebrating life's beauty, no matter how small.

Affirmation & Gratitude

I am grateful for joy, romance, and creativity, trusting play nourishes my spirit and sparks inspiration.

Capricorn
28 December 2026

Work, health, and routines are spotlighted. Capricorn, you may feel the urge to tidy unfinished tasks or refine habits before year's end. The stars encourage balance—don't overburden yourself, but do take steps that create stability. Progress now is about laying groundwork for 2027. By aligning productivity with self-care, you ensure resilience for the year ahead. Today is about sustainable preparation, not rushed effort.

Affirmation & Gratitude

I am grateful for supportive routines that nurture balance, strength, and stability, trusting steady steps prepare me for the year

Capricorn
29 December 2026

Relationships are emphasized. The stars encourage empathy, patience, and honest dialogue. Capricorn, your steadiness provides security, but deeper intimacy grows from vulnerability. A meaningful exchange could heal old rifts or strengthen trust. Today is about valuing love as much as achievement. Bonds nurtured with care now will support you in the year ahead. Harmony requires listening, respect, and openness—qualities you already carry naturally.

Affirmation & Gratitude

I am grateful for love and respect in my relationships, trusting openness creates deeper harmony and connection.

Capricorn
30 December 2026

Shared resources or emotional bonds may surface. The stars highlight trust, fairness, and clarity. Capricorn, you may need to resolve financial matters, boundaries, or emotional entanglements before the year closes. Avoid assumptions—address issues directly to create stability. Emotional honesty also strengthens connection. By facing matters with courage, you close the year with balance and empowerment. Transparency today is preparation for peace tomorrow.

Affirmation & Gratitude

I am grateful for clarity and fairness in shared matters, trusting honesty builds stability and peace.

Capricorn
31 December 2026

The year closes with growth and reflection. Capricorn, the stars encourage you to look back with gratitude and forward with curiosity. Lessons learned in 2026 prepare you for expansion in 2027. This is a day for celebration, but also intention-setting. Embrace both joy and wisdom as you step into the new year. Trust that your path continues to align with your purpose—your foundation is strong, and your spirit is ready.

Affirmation & Gratitude

I am grateful for the wisdom of the past year, trusting curiosity and purpose guide me into the future.

www.ingramcontent.com/pod-product-compliance
Lightning Source LLC
Chambersburg PA
CBHW071145070526